COLD CASE
MUNCIE

DOUGLAS WALKER & KEITH ROYSDON

THE
History
PRESS

Published by The History Press
Charleston, SC
www.historypress.com

CONTENTS

CONTENTS

COLD CASES ARE MARKED
BY HOPE AND DREAD

On a warm day in August 2014, two families watched as investigators from several police departments searched a house on South Council Street in downtown Muncie.

The families waited with a mix of hope and dread because word had spread around town, driven by social media posts, that police had received a tip that a missing woman's remains could be found in the house.

Hope because the families longed for answers. Dread because of what those answers might be.

A crowd had gathered in nearby yards and along sidewalks up and down the block, watching for hours as police walked in and out of the house.

From just outside the yellow crime scene tape strung around the house and its yard, family members of Brianna DiBattiste spoke with high-ranking police officials who, for the most part, were waiting outside while the house was being searched by investigators, some using a police dog.

DiBattiste, a twenty-five-year-old from the town of Dunkirk, just over the county line from Delaware County, in Jay County, had last been seen on June 16.

In the crowd that gathered was another small family group, including the parents of Ashley Morris Mullis, a twenty-eight-year-old mother of three, who had been missing for almost a year, since September 2013.

DiBattiste's remains were ultimately found in a wilderness area in Jay County in September 2014. Authorities and her family came to believe that she had overdosed and her companion, rather than taking her to get medical attention, had abandoned her to die in a stand of trees.

A "dead end" sign near a cold case scene. *Photo by Keith Roysdon.*

As of early 2023, Mullis has not been found. Her family posts on social media about a man she had been dating. The man has since died, and Mullis's family and friends, several of whom turned out for an impromptu vigil that day in August 2014, have repeatedly called for the man's family to help resolve her disappearance.

Mullis's story, and her family's agonized wait for answers, is told in this book. DiBattiste's story is not told at great length in this book because some mysteries surrounding her death have been solved. But their stories differ only by the time their families waited—in one case, are still waiting—for answers. The loss to their loved ones is equally felt.

That's the measure of a cold case, ultimately: the wait for answers, and the toll taken on survivors by the loss of their friend, daughter, son, mother, father or loved one. That toll is at the heart of every unsolved murder or disappearance.

Over the course of nearly ten years in the 2010s, the authors of this book wrote newspaper articles about more than thirty cold cases in the Muncie, Indiana area. A couple of those have been resolved in the years since, with arrests, but most are still open and unsolved.

And families are still waiting for answers.

Cold cases are shockingly common as a percentage of total homicides nationally. That's because the murder clearance rate, the percentage of homicides that are solved, had in 2020 fallen to only about 50 percent, the lowest point in a half century, CBS News reported in mid-2022.

CBS quoted Thomas Harper of the Murder Accountability Project that it was "a 50-50-coin flip" as to whether a homicide would be solved. "It's never been this bad," Harper added.

The human quotient goes beyond the raw numbers.

Andrea Ciriaco, a writer and cold case researcher who contacted the authors of this book seeking help in gathering information about long-unsolved Indiana killings, said unsolved homicides around the United States are fascinating but the impact on survivors is what's telling.

"That's what hooks me, gets me so interested," Ciriaco said in an interview. "It's a puzzle, and if it were solved, it would mean so much to so many people."

In this book you'll find the stories of about two dozen men and women who died violent deaths but whose murders have gone unsolved. For the loved ones of each of those people, the waiting for some resolution has been hard. For some, it's been nearly intolerable.

You'll meet Maggie Mae Fleming, shot to death as she sat by a window in her south-side Muncie home in 1962; Lou Ann Cox, killed in March 1996, her body dumped on the banks of a reservoir; Ruby Dean Moore, found dead on Christmas Eve 1964; Sebastian Cisneros, whose father still wants justice for his son's 2009 killing.

We'll tell you about Paula Garrett, who was killed in 1979. Her young son, Eric, was bludgeoned and critically injured by the attacker who killed his mother. Eric Garrett's life since his childhood has been shaped by his need for justice.

That need for justice—because it's far from certain that answers or even an arrest would truly bring closure to survivors—is a common theme in the stories we'll tell here. In a couple of chapters in this book, we'll talk about the best-case scenario for some families and loved ones of people whose lives were ended: a resolution and an arrest.

There's no end to the hope for survivors that justice might still be done.

No remains were found that day in August 2014. Police ultimately said they were led on a series of wild goose chases by a would-be informant.

For the families who stood by that day—perhaps for several families because we can't be sure who else might have been in the crowd—the search brought no immediate answers.

And few answers have been forthcoming in the years since.

With this book, we hope to bring attention to these cases again, hoping for some bit of information that might close these cases. In each of the chapters that focuses on a specific cold case, we include a point of contact with a police agency for the use of anyone who might have more information.

Because it doesn't matter how much time has passed if justice remains unserved. And even cold justice is better than no justice at all.

ASSASSINATION

Perhaps Maggie Mae Fleming had a premonition concerning the fate that awaited her on the evening of October 6, 1962.

Nearly a half century later, in 2011, Fleming's daughter, Ethel Jean Douthitt, told the *Star Press* her mother had an aversion to people being able to see into their family's home, in Muncie's industry neighborhood, during the evening hours.

Douthitt recalled her mother would tell her, "Ethel Jean, turn off those lights. Shut those curtains. People are crazy out there."

At about 8:00 p.m. on that Saturday night in 1962, Fleming was seated on a couch in her South Grant Street home, holding her four-year-old son, Steven, when someone fired a handgun from outside.

The couch was pushed up against an unused door, and the .38-caliber bullet passed through a glass window in the door and struck the thirty-year-old Fleming in the back of her head. The mother of three children—another son, five-year-old Dwight, was also home at the time—slumped over on the couch and died almost instantly.

Among Muncie killings, it was apparently the rare occurrence of a planned assassination.

Fleming's uncle, Ira "Big Red" Benford, was in the same room when his niece was shot but maintained he didn't see her assailant. Benford raced to two nearby homes—the occupant of the first house he went to refused to open her door—to ask that police be notified.

A newspaper photo capturing the death scene of Maggie Mae Fleming. *Authors' collection.*

Another adult in the house when the shot was fired, described by police at Fleming's twenty-seven-year-old boyfriend, told detectives he was asleep at the time.

At the time of her mother's death, sixteen-year-old Ethel Jean Douthitt was at the downtown Strand Theater, watching *Only Two Can Play*, a romantic comedy starring British comedian Peter Sellers.

When she returned home later in the evening, the house was dark and unoccupied. Douthitt immediately sensed that something terrible had happened to her mother.

During the 2011 interview, Douthitt—at the time of the slaying pregnant and days away from getting married—recalled that detectives at first suggested she might have been behind the homicide in order to collect a $1,500 life insurance payment.

"They insisted I killed my mother," she said. "I think they just wanted to close the case."

However, the teenager passed a lie detector test, and a police detective went to the Strand and watched the Sellers movie, determining Douthitt had provided an accurate account of its plot.

Douthitt said in 2011 detectives for a time suspected her also because of her familiarity with the makes and models of handguns. She said that knowledge came from having spent part of her childhood in a home adjacent to another family member's bootleg alcohol business.

A September 1958 article in the *Muncie Star* reported Maggie Fleming was present when police raided such an operation at an East Willard Street address adjacent to Fleming's home, arresting ten and seizing ninety bottles of beer, along with other alcoholic beverages and "21 empty bottles."

While investigators said there were no indications Fleming had any "bitter" enemies, they for a time focused on one of the slaying victim's former boyfriends.

At the time of her death, Fleming was pursuing legal action against the man over his failure to pay child support. According to one account, a hearing on her complaint was scheduled to be held the week after she died.

(There was also a history of violence in the relationship. In January 1955, the man was convicted of assault and battery stemming from an attack on Fleming. With her right eye still swollen, she later appeared at his sentencing hearing in Muncie City Court and urged the judge to allow the man to continue to visit her home. The judge imposed a one-dollar fine.)

However, the ex-boyfriend was able to persuade Muncie police he was twenty miles from the shooting scene, in New Castle, when the fatal shot was fired.

Detectives questioned numerous witnesses, some described as "reluctant," and took four potential suspects to Indianapolis, where they submitted to lie detector tests. All four passed those exams "with flying colors," according to a newspaper account.

Maggie Fleming, who had moved to Muncie from Mississippi in 1951, was laid to rest at Beech Grove Cemetery.

A year after her slaying, Assistant Police Chief David Thomas told the *Muncie Star* the case was "very much alive, but it's impossible to tell how close we are to solving it."

Apparently not very close, as it turned out. Six decades later, the case remains unsolved. In 2011, a detective told the *Star Press* the city police department did not appear to still have any files related to the Fleming homicide.

With her mother gone, Ethel Jean Douthitt raised her two younger brothers, along with ten other children, both her own offspring and extended family members.

She often thought of her mother over the decades.

"I always thought, 'What would Mama do?' under certain circumstances," Douthitt recalled. "I did a lot of praying."

Her younger brother Steven—on their mother's lap when she died—never got over the loss, his sister said.

October 6, 1962

Local news: Efforts were underway to raise funds so a three-year-old Muncie boy could travel to his native Puerto Rico, where physicians said they could perform an operation to remove a tumor from the youngster's brain. The child would survive until 1970.

The month of September 1962 would also see residents of Muncie, and elsewhere, fearing an imminent nuclear attack as the Cuban Missile Crisis unfolded.

Music: "Sherry," by the Four Seasons, dominated the popular music charts in October 1962.

And while they were still more than a year away from topping the charts in the United States, four young musicians who called themselves The Beatles released their first single in their native England, "Love Me Do."

TV: *The Beverly Hillbillies*, which had debuted on September 26, 1962, quickly became America's most-watched TV series, earning some of the highest ratings ever for a thirty-minute situation comedy.

Movies: *The Wonderful World of the Brothers Grimm* would succeed *The Music Man* as Americans' top-rated motion picture in early October 1962.

Books: *Ship of Fools* by Katherine Anne Porter was the best-selling fiction book in the United States.

"It just tore him up inside," she remembered.

In 1990, Steven, known to friends as "Big Easy," was shot during an argument with another man in the Munsyana Homes public housing complex. He survived that wound but died about a decade later, of a heart attack, when he was forty-three.

For most of her adult life, Douthitt continued to believe it was likely that the ex-boyfriend her mother was pursuing child support from had been somehow responsible for the 1962 killing.

When she once confronted the man with her suspicions, Douthitt said, his response was "What are you talking about?"

But years later, an acquaintance approached Douthitt and told her a woman, with ties to her mother's ex-boyfriend and jealous of his continued dealings with Maggie Fleming, had confessed to the killing while on her deathbed.

Another person later told Douthitt that children in the neighborhood—where Fleming's home, and others in the 600 block of South Grant Street, have long since been demolished—had seen an assailant on the night of the murder but were persuaded by their family members to not get involved.

Yet another source told members of the Fleming family that a stranger had checked into a nearby boardinghouse shortly before the homicide and was never seen again after the slaying.

"I didn't have any closure," Douthitt recalled. "And then I got too many closures."

If You Have Information

If you have information that could help an investigation into this cold case, contact the Muncie Police Department. Police chief Nate Sloan asks that you contact the Criminal Investigations Division of the Muncie Police Department at 765-747-4867.

"WE KNOW HE DID IT.
WE JUST CAN'T PROVE IT"

What Is a Cold Case?

The most basic definition of a cold case is a crime unsolved by police investigators. Usually, the phrase is applied to unsolved killings or at least life-ending foul play in which the guilty party goes unpunished.

In *The Westside Park Murders*, the 2021 book from The History Press by the authors of this book, the 1985 slaying of two teenagers in Westside Park in Muncie, Indiana, is cited as probably the most notorious in the city's history.

But every unsolved slaying hangs around the neck of survivors and often investigators, like a heavy stone, sometimes for decades. Sometimes there's some relief when a suspect is punished for another crime, as in the Westside Park case. Sometimes there's a feeling of closure when a mystery is resolved. Sometimes there is no closure, if that's even possible in these cases.

Untold millions of people carry the weight of unsolved killings. How many unsolved murders are on the books in the United States? According to Project Cold Case, about 185,000 cases of homicide and nonnegligent manslaughter went unsolved from 1980 to 2019. That number is based on a Scripps Howard News Service analysis of the FBI's Uniform Crime Report.

And the clearance rate is getting worse. The national average is about 50 percent of murders solved. Indiana's clearance rate was only about 45 percent from 2015 to 2020, according to CBS. Project Cold Case's reporting indicates a better number for Indiana: 59 percent of 17,523 homicides solved. The remaining 7,205 were unsolved.

The house where Robert Nelson was killed. *Photo by Keith Roysdon.*

Project Cold Case, founded in 2015, has been approached by families and investigators on more than 1,000 unsolved murders. The website publishes cold case stories to help bring attention to them. The website cites an overall percent of 66 percent of 947,521 homicides between 1965 and 2019 solved.

The CBS report notes, "In the late 1960s and 1970s, police reported solving about seven of every 10 murders. In 2020, they only solved half." Black victims' murders are less likely to be solved.

The uncertainty—for friends, family and investigators—is among the heaviest burdens anyone can carry.

Asked if any unsolved murders had stuck with him over the decades, veteran Delaware County police investigator Jerry Cook in 2022 recalled a case from 1990 that isn't classified as a cold case—and isn't even classified as a homicide, although Cook is certain it was one.

On May 30, 1990, Jon Phillip Faust left the Mark III, a downtown Muncie bar. Faust was accompanied by another man who had been hanging out at the bar for a couple of weeks.

As far as authorities know, Faust was never seen again after he left the bar.

Faust's roommate reported him missing the next day. His father said he didn't know where his son had gone.

According to police reports, the bartender who remembered Faust leaving the bar found Faust's car, parked not far away, two days later.

"We checked his apartment, and there had been a struggle," Cook said. "The guy he was seen leaving with went to Florida. He got arrested for rolling a guy in Florida. [Veteran investigator] Bob Crabbs and I got in a car and went to Florida and [the suspect] was talkative until we mentioned [Faust]. He clammed up when we asked him.

"We know he did it. We just can't prove it. And nobody saw [Faust] again."

Eric Hoffman, who began his second term as Delaware County prosecutor in January 2023 but whose career as a deputy prosecutor goes back twenty years, said cold cases remain in his mind—and in his files.

"I keep a list," Hoffman said in an interview. "It goes back to the '70s or '80s. It's not all of Delaware County's cold cases and I just keep a small file on each one."

"I occasionally go back to the police departments and see where they are on each case," Hoffman added. "I like the intellectual challenge of them, of digging into a cold case. But the best thing of all is when you can finally put a case together and meet with a family and tell them, 'This is who we believe killed your loved one. We don't even get into the facts of the case, or tell them the suspect's name if charges haven't been filed."

Hoffman remembers in particular meeting with the family of Teresa French, who was killed in Muncie in May 1993. It wasn't until the late 2000s that her killer, Jess David Woods, was arrested. He had killed her after being hired by French's estranged husband.

"Her sister never thought she would see justice," Hoffman said.

"I opened up an investigation once we got evidence. We kept it so tight, only a few knew we were actively investigating it. I didn't even tell the family until the suspect was in custody in our jail.

"All that emotion that poured out when I told them was quite something."

"I've seen cases that just seemed to linger on, and the effect it has on… families," said Judge Marianne Vorhees, who retired from the Delaware Circuit Court bench at the end of 2022. "They really do want to have some kind of endpoint. On sentencing day, they're so relieved it's over."

Andrea Ciriaco has seen firsthand the impact that a cold case has on families. A writer and researcher originally from Ohio, Ciriaco has worked with the family of Ann Harmeier, a twenty-year-old woman Indiana University student killed in September 1977. Harmeier's killer has never been charged.

"It's a puzzle," Ciriaco said. "And if it were solved, it would mean so much to so many people.

"It's just a story to us, but [for] loved ones, family members and friends, it's important for us to remember them as part of the history," she said.

For retired investigators like Cook, the need to tackle cold cases is easily explained.

"It's closure," Cook said. "Nobody likes to leave anything undone. You don't like to do half a job. The officers don't want to give up. That's why everybody is hot about cold cases.

"In most cases, they can be solved. You might not solve it this week, but months from now, somebody could call and give you the information you need to clear a case. Or sometimes more than one."

A YOUNG MOTHER'S BRUTAL SLAYING

Children of the 1970s share many fond memories of their growing up: *Star Wars* movies, collecting pop bottles to return for deposit and summer, when the days stretched out ahead as if warm nights would never end.

For Eric Garrett, those carefree days ended early, when he was only four years old. They ended on March 24, 1979, when a man beat his mother to death and bludgeoned Eric so badly the boy was left with nine skull fractures and permanent disabilities.

Paula Garrett, just twenty-two, was killed by the man she was dating at the time, her son believes.

Eric has spent much of the forty-plus years since his mother's murder looking for justice.

He's spent all of it without his mother.

Eric almost always wears a ball cap to cover the scars and dents on his head from when he was beaten. When he shakes hands, the fingers on his right hand are numb and curled. He is easygoing in conversation and in posting humorous memes on social media.

He's not easygoing when it comes to the murder of the young woman who brought him into the world. He's written a book, *Unprosecuted: My Mother's Murder and the Search for Accountability*. He's tirelessly asked police and prosecutors to review the case. He believes one man—a man who was arrested shortly after Paula Garrett's murder but ultimately released—killed his mother and must pay for the crime.

Paula and Eric Garrett. *Provided by family.*

And he's angry at authorities who haven't pursued the case.

"We had all the evidence," Eric said in a 2022 interview for this book. "There was way more evidence than what was needed.

"I blame a lot of people" for the lack of prosecution, he added. "I'm just being honest."

Paula Garrett had gotten pregnant with Eric when she was still a student at Muncie's Southside High School. Eric was born a few days after she finished her senior year. She had married and divorced Eric's father, and she worked as a waitress at Jane's Restaurant, a popular diner on the south side, just one hundred yards from where two major city streets, Walnut and Madison, cross.

A gas station stood nearby, a junkyard was just a bit farther down the road and Muncie's then-thriving Kmart store was across the street.

Jane's was owned by Paula's aunt and was the kind of place that attracted truckers, farmers from Cowan and other areas south of the city and police officers. Paula always greeted her customers with a smile, and they liked her, this woman who stood just over five feet tall and weighed only about one hundred pounds.

Paula and Eric lived in a duplex on Primrose Lane on Muncie's south side, the part of town where most of the city's blue-collar workers called home. Paula's boyfriend, Richard Green, was thirty-six years old and married. That night, March 24, 1979, Green had visited, and they watched a ball game on TV. Green apparently left for a while, came back and left in the early-morning hours.

After Green was ostensibly gone, Eric crawled into bed with his mother. At some point, Eric remembered, Green came back to the bedroom and flipped on the light.

Sometime after 1:30 a.m., Green and Mary Bicknell, Paula's mother, checked the duplex because Bicknell hadn't heard from her daughter. Green said he hadn't heard from Paula either.

Paula, wearing a purple dressing gown and heart-shaped pendant necklace, lay on the bed, curled into an almost fetal position. Eric was on the floor. The mother and son had suffered massive head trauma from beatings with a blunt object. Paula was dead. Eric's skull was fractured in nine places, but he was breathing.

Green told police that Paula's ex-boyfriend, Merle Huffman, had been causing "trouble" for the young woman.

Because authorities thought Eric would die from his injuries, a police officer rode with the boy in an ambulance to Methodist Hospital in Indianapolis, hoping he might be able to say who beat him and killed his mother.

Eric recovered from his serious injuries and identified Green as the attacker. The boy had not yet turned five years old.

In the weeks following Paula Garrett's death, Richard Green was arrested. In a court hearing to determine if he should be released on bond, one of Paula's neighbors said they had seen Green hurriedly walking away from the duplex the night of the murder. Other neighbors said it was common to hear Green and Paula arguing.

A videotaped interview with Eric was played in the courtroom. When asked who killed his mother and attacked him, Eric said, "Richard… Richard Green."

Delaware Circuit Court Judge Steven Caldemeyer denied Green's release on bond.

As time passed, police investigators took Green to Chicago for a lie detector test, apparently the latest in a series. He passed the test but hadn't been informed of that by the police investigators, so he gave them the slip while in the city. The next day, after Green heard that he had passed, he called Muncie police, who went back to Chicago to pick him up and bring him back to Muncie.

"I always thought that was bullshit," Jerry Cook, a veteran Delaware County police investigator, said in a 2022 interview for this book. "You don't keep giving someone a lie detector test until they pass it." Green had failed at least a couple of polygraph tests in Muncie before he was taken to Chicago for the test, Cook said. He acknowledged he was not involved in the Garrett investigation. "She was my third cousin."

Police investigators years later disagreed in their opinions of Green's guilt. They weren't the only ones. Police chief Richard Heath said Green was a suspect and would remain one.

But Muncie police were feuding with Delaware County prosecutor Michael "Mick" Alexander and had been for months. A later lawsuit produced testimony that reflected that a business associate of Green had facilitated contact between the prosecutor's office and the Chicago lie detector operator. Decades later, in an interview with the authors of this

Left: Eric Garrett in 2022. *Photo by Keith Roysdon.*

Right: The cover of Eric Garrett's book about his mother. *Scanned cover.*

book for a cold case article, Alexander said that he, and only he, had made decisions in his office's handling of the case.

Those decisions included not prosecuting Richard Green.

In an interview a few years before he died in 2017, Alexander expressed little hope that the case would ever be resolved.

"It would take a confession" to close the Garrett case, he said in the interview.

With little effort, Eric Garrett can recount the facts of the case that ultimately didn't lead to a prosecution and conviction.

"We had twenty-two bags of blood-soaked evidence, with nail scrapings and everything, and they said they lost it in a flood," he said in a 2022 interview. (Another chapter in this book covers that same circumstance.)

"Friends asked people who have worked at city hall forever, and they said they had never heard of that."

"Evidence was sent to the state police," he added. "They should have all the blood types. All of it's gone. I had a friend who was a state police officer who tried to look into it and couldn't find anything."

As for the authorities in charge, Garrett said, "You can't believe anything they say.

"I'm a little bitter, but it's the truth. I try not to act like an asshole, but you know…the proof is in the pudding."

Does he believe that investigations like the one into his mother's killing stall because of inertia or because someone is protecting someone?

"A little bit of both."

"I want to go to court," he said. "I want to take Richard Green to court."

Eric said he wrote his book, which came out in 2019, because "I just wanted to bring more attention to my mother's case."

At forty-eight, Eric has lived more than twice as long as his mother did. He usually doesn't post on Facebook about his mother's death, but his posts—like his conversation—sometimes show a wry sadness that he earned early in his life.

Does he hear from people who want him to stop talking about his mother's killing?

"Nobody's ever come up and said, quit talking about this. I've had some dirty looks. Nobody's ever threatened me, but I stay home, I don't go out.

"I'm sure there is a lot of people that want me to shut up."

Eric Garrett shares a trait with many other cold case survivors: a somber unwillingness to give up and go away.

He said he'd like to hear from other survivors who know what he's been going through since he was a child. "I'd love for that to happen."

Before writing a 2014 newspaper article about Paula Garrett's killing, the authors of this book accompanied Eric Garrett to the scene of the crime: the Primrose Lane duplex where his mother was killed and he was so badly beaten he sustained lifelong injuries.

The owner and landlord of the duplex, after apparently recognizing Eric, walked up and said that renewed publicity about the case would have a negative impact on her ability to find tenants for the building. She told Eric that the crime had happened "a long time ago."

Bad publicity would hurt the duplex's rental potential, she said, "especially in this economy." She then asked Garrett to put himself in her shoes. "Do you have any rentals?"

In an effort to find Green to ask him for comment for the 2014 article, the authors used the address on a recent traffic ticket to seek him out at a rural home southeast of Muncie. A man at the address said Green didn't live there but sometimes drove a commercial vehicle for him.

MARCH 24, 1979

Local news: In local news on this date, former Muncie Community Development assistant director Anthony G. Burrus faced charges resulting from an FBI investigation and indictment by a federal grand jury. He testified that the $200 he received from a contractor was neither the result of extortion by him nor a bribe from the contractor. The Central High School Bearcats basketball team was preparing to try to win its seventh state championship. And police were looking for two young white males who held up the White Flash gas station in Yorktown.

Music: The top hit song on the *Billboard* charts for the week of March 24, 1979, was "Tragedy" by the Bee Gees.

Movies: *The China Syndrome*, the thriller about a near-meltdown at a California nuclear plant, was the top movie at the box office from March 21 to April 18, 1979.

TV: The top-rated TV shows of the week ending March 25, 1979, were *Three's Company, Mork & Mindy* and *Laverne & Shirley.*

Books: The top *New York Times* bestseller for the week ending March 25, 1979, was Herman Wouk's *War and Remembrance*, the sequel to *The Winds of War.*

As the man spoke, two other men came out of a nearby barn and stood as if to back up Green's boss.

"I can't imagine he would want to talk to you," the first man said.

It was impossible to tell if one of the men who confronted the authors that day was Green.

Eric said in 2022 that he's not sure he'd recognize Richard Green today.

"Last time I heard, he lived a few blocks away from me," he said. "He's in his seventies. I think I might have seen him a couple of times. I know I saw him in the late '80s or early '90s. I probably wouldn't recognize him now."

Eric said he was grateful for any attention that could be drawn to his mother's murder but acknowledged that getting justice has been an uphill battle.

"It's not just the evil of people that do that. It's the officials that allow it to go on without repercussions. Not just in my case. It's rampant. And I don't think it's gonna stop."

If You Have Information

If you have information that could help an investigation into this cold case, contact the Muncie Police Department. Police chief Nate Sloan asks that you contact the Criminal Investigations Division of the Muncie Police Department at 765-747-4867.

A DAUGHTER REMEMBERS

Beth Miller turned seven years old the day after her father's body was found in a vacant lot in Dunkirk, Indiana.

To say that her life since May 1973 has been marked by a desire for justice is an understatement.

Now, a half a century after Albert Milton Miller—known as Billy to those who knew him—was killed, the fact that his killer was never punished for the crime is still a weight Beth Miller and her siblings carry with them.

They also carry the feeling that their father's murder is all but forgotten in this Jay County town.

"I don't hear anything about it," Beth Miller said. "A lot of people who were around then are gone now. We don't talk much about it."

Beth is a substitute teacher, and she and her husband are busy with Paisley, their youngest. A preschooler, Paisley is too young to know about her grandfather's murder.

When that time comes, Paisley might be about the same age as Beth was when she heard the news.

Bill Miller was a bit of a hell-raiser who, along with running buddy David Gordon Garrett, tooled around the backroads and side streets of Dunkirk and Muncie and everywhere between. The two would show up after a late-night run and have everything from hams to tools to circus tickets that they would give to family members.

Police knew that the two friends were sometimes on the ragged edge of the law, but Miller, in particular, was well-liked.

Bill Miller. *Photo provided by family.*

Then on the night of May 9, 1973, Bill Miller felt the point-blank brunt of a shotgun blast and was left to die, in a vacant lot in Dunkirk.

Garrett, his running buddy, left town, driving a red 1958 Chevy pickup truck. He was accompanied by his ten-year-old son.

Garrett was arrested a few days later in Richmond and, later in May 1973, a grand jury indicted him on a charge of murder.

He went to trial in New Castle, in nearby Henry County, and was promptly found not guilty.

It's not like there was much mystery to Bill Miller's murder. David Gordon Garrett's wife, Naomi, told police her husband confessed.

"I did a bad thing last night," Garrett told Naomi. "And I will probably feel bad about it for a few months. I killed Bill Miller last night."

Naomi Garrett told police that her husband and Garrett, who were both thirty-nine years old, had for more than a year been breaking into places and stealing items—in between stops for diet pills at the Muncie office of physician Jules LaDuron. (LaDuron's long and sometimes controversial life is covered in *Muncie Murder & Mayhem*, a 2018 book by the authors of this book that's available from The History Press.)

Garrett was reportedly mad at Miller after seeing a newspaper article about a break-in at a finance company office. "I told Miller that was my hit," Naomi Garrett quoted her husband as saying. "I am going to have to stomp him."

Garrett told his wife Bill Miller's last words: "Garrett, you SOB."

Naomi Garrett's statements to police varied from her frank recitation of her husband's confession to another version in which, after he and Miller were confronted in the middle of burglarizing a building, he ran and heard shots ring out behind him, where Miller remained.

While Garrett was still on the road with his son, a friend told him that police were looking for him.

"What for? There been a death in the family or something?" Garrett replied. When the friend told him that Miller's body had been found, Garrett asked, "Who put them on me?"

Gerald Kirby was a young cop in 1973 and later became Dunkirk's police chief and then Jay County sheriff. In a 2013 article about the Miller cold case written by the authors of this book, he recalled his surprise that the 1974 trial ended with Garrett's acquittal. He added that some witnesses contradicted their previous statements to police.

When it came to Bill Miller and David Gordon Garrett, Kirby recalled in 2013: "The wrong one died."

But the biggest twist in the wake of Bill Miller's death didn't come until 2013. After he was acquitted of killing Bill Miller, David Gordon Garrett became a familiar name to law enforcement officers in East Central Indiana. For the 2013 article, veteran Delaware County police investigator Jerry Cook recalled, "Every time you turned around, Garrett was getting arrested for something. It was usually burglaries or fights or being drunk. Dave was one of those guys you could count on, after a weekend, seeing his name on the jail log."

Garrett spent two years in prison on a burglary conviction in Kentucky and had a Delaware County conviction on his record as late as 2000.

Over the years after they became adults, Beth Miller and her sister, Debbie, began to look into the circumstances of their father's murder and Garrett's

Beth Miller and her daughter, Paisley. *Photo by Keith Roysdon.*

MAY 9, 1973

Local news: Indiana senator Birch Bayh was in town for what was billed as a "nonpolitical" public forum. Bayh expressed concerns about "cynicism and disenchantment" of many Americans. Area farmers worried about a shortage of propane gas for use in drying grain from the fall harvest.

Music: "Tie a Yellow Ribbon Round the Ole Oak Tree" by Tony Orlando and Dawn was the top hit on the *Billboard* charts for the week.

Movies: The top movie for two weeks leading up to the date was *Soylent Green*, the Charlton Heston/Edward G. Robinson science-fiction thriller about a dystopian future when a shortage of food prompts some unusual corporate offerings.

TV: Cliff Robertson starred in *The Man Without a Country*, the top-rated TV movie of the period. Two new TV series, *Kung Fu* and *Barnaby Jones*, also fared well in the ratings.

Books: Jacqueline Susann's latest steamy novel, *Once Is Not Enough*, topped the *New York Times* bestseller list for all of May and June.

acquittal. They got copies of trial documents from the Henry County courthouse and copies of old newspaper articles from the library. In the process of their research, they found a half brother in California they didn't know they had.

They also placed a cross and later planted a rosebush on the lot where their father's body had been found.

"We've always thought about him," Debbie Miller told the authors for the 2013 article. "We always thought Dave killed him and got away with it."

But the siblings and their mother tried to find some peace in the aftermath of Bill Miller's death.

The sisters contacted the authors of this book in 2013, asking if their father's case might be the subject of one of a series of cold case articles that began appearing in the *Star Press* newspaper in 2010.

As work on the article began, Beth Miller called with some shocking news: David Gordon Garrett had died at age seventy-nine.

Garrett's family members who spoke to the authors said they had experienced uncertainty over the forty years since Bill Miller's death and their father's trial.

That was not the reaction of Bill Miller's children.

"The first thing that entered my mind was, 'He got away with it all over again,'" Beth Miller said in 2013. "He had lived for forty years, and a few weeks before he might have to answer some questions (for the article)…I was hoping he might answer some questions.

"I know he's had to answer to God, but I wanted him to answer to us first," she said.

Miller did note that she's felt sympathy for Garrett's children.

"They're victims too. You still love your dad, no matter what. I don't blame them because their dad killed our dad. This affects a lot of people. It hurts a lot of people that are innocent, all because of one guilty person."

In a 2022 interview, Beth Miller was philosophical about the fifty years that have passed since her father's murder.

Her time is occupied with Paisley, who squirms and smiles and laughs like any almost-four-year-old while her mom talks about things kids couldn't begin to understand. Beth wants to keep teaching until her daughter is out of elementary school. She wants to travel.

Her father's story and the story of his death is known by her older son and by her grandson.

"It's passed on through the generations, something like this," she said. "Sometimes you try not to put that dark cloud over your kids, but somebody in the family gets hold of it and it goes on for generations."

Beth Miller has pictures of her father, and she'll share them with Paisley someday.

"We have his pictures, for when she's old enough to ask."

MURDER AT THE MAPLES MOTEL

While her final years were plagued by cocaine abuse, Lou Ann Cox had known better times.

Cox—who was forty-two when she was murdered in March 1996—for a significant portion of her life had been known as a hard worker at jobs that included cleaning local homes.

She also kept herself almost impeccably clean, Cox's mother, Mary Oxley, told the *Star Press* in 2011.

Oxley called her daughter a "pleasant lady" with "beautiful red hair." She also enjoyed collecting Pepsi memorabilia.

The collapse of her marriage in the late 1980s seemed to throw Cox's life into turmoil, family members said.

"She was always so clean," her mother recalled. "But then she went the other way, and she didn't take care of herself at all. The last time I saw her, she looked terrible."

Oxley said after her daughter was seriously injured in a traffic accident, her dependence on drugs, and her dealings with other drug abusers, increased.

Cox repeatedly asked her mother for cash.

To avoid funding drug purchases, Oxley took to buying the items, most often food and gasoline, her daughter said she needed.

Family members also noticed Cox was selling off mementos that had been part of her once cherished Pepsi memorabilia collection.

In 1995, when her father was in the final stages of a terminal illness, Cox was arrested for possession of cocaine. Her life appeared to be in free fall.

Left: Lou Ann Cox. *Photo provided by family*.

Below: A police car at Prairie Creek Reservoir during the Lou Ann Cox investigation. *From the authors' collection*.

"In that last year, I didn't see her too much," her mother said.

About 11:30 a.m. on Saturday, March 9, 1996, a worker at Prairie Creek Reservoir observed that someone had dumped something in weeds, not far from motorcycle trails on the reservoir's southwest side.

The park employee was stunned a few minutes later when he determined that object was actually a woman's nude body, wrapped in two blankets. Her face appeared battered and swollen.

Late that night, the victim was identified as Lou Ann Cox by a family member who recognized the Pepsi tattoo on her left ankle.

James St. Myer, at that time the Delaware County coroner, said an autopsy revealed Cox had died as a result of "strangulation by ligature." He suggested the murder weapon might have been a thin rope or wire.

Two days after the body was discovered, employees of the Maples Motel—a group of small cabins, along Old Indiana 67 south of Muncie, available for overnight lodging—reported a blanket was missing from one of the cabins, which also contained a bloodstained mattress.

Records showed Cox had checked into another cabin at the Maples property early on the morning of March 8, turning in her key the following evening.

About 3:30 a.m. on March 9—approximately eight hours before her body would be discovered—Cox returned to the roadside motel and asked for the key to the same cabin but was turned away.

An employee reported that despite not being given a key, Cox was last seen walking in the darkness in the direction of that cabin.

DNA tests would later determine the blood found on the mattress at the Maples was indeed that of Cox. No other person's DNA was recovered from the scene.

Muncie police later interviewed a local man who had stayed at the Maples motel that night and also acknowledged that he knew the slaying victim. The questioning ended, however, when the man asserted his right to consult with an attorney.

"I feel certain he knows something about it," Terry Winters, at the time the city's deputy police chief, told the *Muncie Evening Press*.

However, investigators found no evidence linking that man—who would die of cancer in 2004—to Cox's death. He was never arrested or formally charged.

City police also found no connection between Cox's death and that of twenty-six-year-old Kim Weatherspoon, found strangled in her East Jackson Street apartment a month before Cox's slaying.

Investigators had noted both homicide victims had a history of drug-related arrests.

(A man linked to Weatherspoon through DNA testing later stood trial for her killing but was found not guilty. He did, however, spend several years in prison after he was convicted in 1998 of breaking into a Ball State University's student home and assaulting her.)

Muncie police also investigated reports Lou Ann Cox had exchanged angry words with a fellow patron in the Village Inn, 2221 East Jackson Street, about 1:30 a.m. on the morning she died.

MARCH 9, 1996

Local news: At a hearing before the state board of tax commissioners, Delaware County clerk Richard Amburn, for many years a critic of government spending, expressed support for a bond issue to fund construction of a new juvenile detention center.

Music: "Not Gon' Cry" by Mary J. Blige topped the Cash Box list of top singles for the week.

TV: *Seinfeld* was at the top of TV ratings in the United States. Other programs drawing high viewership included *Friends* and *ER*.

Movies: *The Birdcage*, which opened on March 8, was the month's most popular film in movie theaters.

Books: *Primary Colors*, seemingly based on the peccadilloes of President Bill Clinton and whose author was identified only later as Joe Klein, was at the top of fiction bestsellers from mid-February through mid-April.

At least one account indicated Cox had slapped that man in the face.

In 2011, a city police detective confirmed investigators had received at least two tips concerning that man's identity. However, he said no related evidence had been uncovered linking anyone to Cox.

Fifteen years after her daughter's death, Mary Oxley said people still occasionally approached her and asked if the killer had ever been brought to justice.

Sadly, Oxley died, at age eighty-three in May 2014, without ever receiving answers about her daughter's death.

She was laid to rest in Muncie's Elm Ridge Cemetery next to her husband. Their daughter is buried nearby—with a tombstone that features a Pepsi logo.

In recent years, the scene of Cox's slaying has also passed into history. The Maples Motel was finally demolished after falling into disrepair following decades of neglect.

Its best days recalled an era when motorists on long trips used two-lane state highways, not four-lane interstates and bypasses.

Its worst day produced the lasting memories associated with the unsolved killing of a local resident.

IF YOU HAVE INFORMATION

If you have information that could help the investigation into this cold case, contact the Delaware County Sheriff's Office. Sheriff Tony Skinner asks that you go to www.delawarecountysheriff.com and click on the CONTACT tab to find telephone numbers to call as well as a contact form that can be filled out anonymously.

DEATH ON "THE CORNER"

The aftermath of Muncie businessman Bill Gump's murder in June 1974 is testimony to the lasting power of secrets.

Not only did people who might have had information germane to the investigation decline to come forward in the summer of 1974, but people were reluctant to talk when the authors of this book wrote a cold case article about Gump in November 2011.

That reluctance, even nearly forty years after the fact, was obvious in comments of Elmer "Fudd" Ashley, who operated a store across from Gump's liquor store at the corner of Willard and Hackley Streets.

Ashley, a veteran local business owner as well as the probation officer for Delaware Superior Court 1 judge Robert Barnet Jr. for twenty years, was reluctant to talk about things he remembered from the time of the killing.

Asked about a possible motive for the killing of the well-liked and respected Gump, Ashley replied, "I don't know. You heard rumors. I don't spread rumors because it could all be wrong."

Gump's murder is unsolved, and no one has ever been charged in connection with the crime.

In the summer of 1974, the corner of Willard and Hackley was a place that could be described as "happening."

Others described it as "trouble prone."

The neighborhood around the street corner was largely Black. Ashley's business in 1974, the Black Bag, catered to young African American men and women in the neighborhood, selling record albums and African dashikis and art.

The scene, in 2022, of Bill Gump's former store. *Photo by Keith Roysdon.*

A 1976 article in the *Muncie Evening Press* called Willard and Hackley "the Corner." Among the businesses at the corner were the liquor store, a bar, a dance hall and a poolroom, Deputy Chief Joe Rowe said.

"At any time, day or night, chances are you could find about anything you wanted: drugs, alcohol, fights, one-night stands, almost any kind of action," according to the article.

Ed Faulkner, owner of Faulkner Mortuary, a long-established Black-owned business, said he was reluctant to schedule funeral calling hours in the evening because so many people were afraid to be in the area after dark.

Six years before that article, earlier newspaper coverage of the neighborhood was decried by a local Black minister, Reverend J.C. Williams, as being primarily from the point of view of police.

Members of the local Black Coalition said that the liquor store at the corner was the primary source of problems in the neighborhood.

"The guys get drunk and cause trouble; then they always blame it on the Black Bag," one member of the coalition said.

An air of antagonism developed between Muncie police and young Black residents of the neighborhood.

At the center of the controversy was the liquor store owned by Bill Gump, who was white.

Considering the number of fingers pointed at Gump, people nevertheless said that he was well-liked by the community.

In reporter Warren Collier's account of Gump's murder, one patron of the store said, "There was nothing wrong with that man. He was good. He did a lot of people a lot of favors. I don't know why anybody would want to shoot him."

Gump's relationship with the customers who frequented the Corner didn't prevent his death on June 14, 1974, however.

For years before Gump was killed, when his store made headlines, it was because it had been robbed or someone going and coming from the store had been robbed or assaulted.

Gump himself had been injured on New Year's Day 1970 when he received a "superficial" stab wound from an assailant at his store. It was the third of three stabbings in the area, presumably by the same knife-wielding man, in a single evening. In June 1970, someone set Gump's car, a yellow Volkswagen, ablaze outside the store.

Gump was well-known in Muncie not only from his liquor store but also from his former ownership of the Green Point Tavern, Cozy Lodge and the 67 Supper Club.

On the night he was killed, Gump was shot twice when he went behind the counter to retrieve some merchandise. Police received an anonymous call around midnight that Gump had been shot. Police found him lying facedown clutching a .25-caliber pistol.

Within a few days, a $1,000 reward—collected from Gump's friends and quickly increased to $2,000—had been offered for information. Lie detector tests were to be administered to three people in the area that night.

But police acknowledged they had "no known suspects in mind."

Within a couple of weeks, police said they were tracing a "Saturday Night Special"—a slang term for a handgun—they felt might have been connected to Gump's murder.

A few months after Gump's slaying, local authorities sought a crackdown on activity on the Corner. In October 1974, the county Alcoholic Beverage Commission said it would not renew the liquor retailer license for the store, now named the Willard Street Package Store, instead voting to place the permit—held by Gump's widow, Catherine—in escrow. Catherine Gump had sought approval to sell the license and the store property to a former local teacher, Fred Ginther.

JUNE 14, 1974

Local news: The *Muncie Star* reported that the Delaware County coroner's office was not filing copies of its coroner's reports with the county clerk's office as required under state law. The newspaper noted that the reports had not been filed in more than three years.

Music: "Billy, Don't Be a Hero" by Bo Donaldson and the Heywoods was the top hit for the week, according to *Billboard*.

Movies: The top box-office movie the week of June 14, 1974, was the reissue of *The Poseidon Adventure*. Among new movies, *The Sting* and *The Lords of Flatbush* were at the top in the weeks immediately before and after.

TV: The Telly Savalas police drama *Kojak* replaced *All in the Family* as the top-rated TV series.

Books: *Watership Down*, Richard Adams's epic tale of a quest by a group of rabbits, was the *New York Times* bestseller for most of May, June and July 1974.

The ABC board wanted any liquor sales stemming from the permit to be moved away from the area.

"There have been more serious and minor crimes at the premises than any other place in the city of Muncie," police chief Cordell Campbell told the ABC board. Campbell said three out of five murders committed in the city in the previous year had occurred at the site.

Attorney Wayne Lennington, representing would-be owner Ginther, asked why objections to the store had never been raised at previous annual liquor license renewals.

The liquor license was, in November 1974, transferred to a different owner and location, set for Wheeling Avenue south of McGalliard Road.

It was the beginning of a downturn in activity for the neighborhood, as reported within a couple of years.

Members of Penn Street Church of Christ bought the building where Gump's liquor store had been. The church later changed its name to the Midtown Church of Christ and bought the building where the Black Bag had been located. The building was still, in 2022, identified as a church by a sign on the side of the structure.

The building where Bill Gump's liquor store was located, which had housed several businesses over the years since his death, appeared mostly unused in the summer of 2022.

IF YOU HAVE INFORMATION

If you have information that could help an investigation into this cold case, contact the Muncie Police Department. Police chief Nate Sloan asks that you contact the Criminal Investigations Division of the Muncie Police Department at 765-747-4867.

STAIRWAY TO HEAVEN

Among the victims of unsolved slayings in Muncie and Delaware County, Joni Michelle Brooks left behind a different kind of legacy in that words she put to paper remain available for review more than two decades after her death.

A New Castle native born in 1955, Brooks spent her early years in the small Henry County town of Sulphur Springs before moving to Muncie in her mid-teens.

She graduated from Northside High School and later earned a nursing degree, working for a time at Ball Memorial Hospital.

She also married and would be remembered as a loving, devoted mother to her five children.

In May 1987, Brooks accidentally fell from her family's van as it traveled down a city street, striking her head on the pavement.

She regained consciousness after a week and remained hospitalized for a month. Friends and family members would later suggest that due to the brain injury suffered in that fall, Brooks was never again the person she had been before the accident.

Prior to her 1987 fall, Joni Brooks had never been charged with a crime. The next dozen years would see her arrested nearly twenty times.

In June 1991, Brooks was arrested at the Munsyana Homes public housing complex after she offered to purchase crack cocaine from two undercover police officers.

At a trial that December, the Muncie woman's mother would describe her daughter's behavior problems since suffering the head injury four

The road where Joni Brooks's body was found. *Photo by Keith Roysdon.*

years earlier. (Court records reflect the mother's repeated efforts to try to help Brooks address the problems stemming from her brain injury and substance abuse.)

After a Delaware Superior Court jury found Brooks guilty of dealing in cocaine, Judge Robert Barnet Jr. imposed a six-year sentence, at the time the minimum penalty for the Class B felony conviction.

A year later, after receiving reports of Brooks's good behavior and rehabilitation efforts in prison, the judge agreed to allow her to spend the remainder of her sentence on probation.

"I want to say that I'm thankful to you for taking me off the streets and away from access to drugs," Brooks had written to the judge from prison. "I've had a lot of time to think and re-evaluate my life."

But within a few weeks of her December 1992 release, a test conducted by a probation officer revealed Brooks had ingested cocaine.

"I didn't have enough strength or will-power to say no," Brooks wrote in a letter to Barnet after the failed drug test. "It was nothing I planned to do. It just happened."

Over the next few years, she would at times return to jail after being accused of violating the terms of her probation or committing relatively minor crimes.

Some of those arrests were for prostitution, a potentially lethal occupation turned to by some to feed their drug addiction.

At times Brooks would enter drug treatment programs and, in one case, a medical facility that specialized in treatment of brain injuries.

"I believe much of Ms. Brooks' pathological behavior in the last years is a direct result of her traumatic brain injury," a clinical neuropsychologist reported to Barnet in November 1993.

When she was asked to describe her problems for a 1994 medical report, Brooks said, "I can't remember anything….I can't handle money at all, and I'm real impulsive with it."

That year also saw Brooks back in jail for probation violations tied to a drug relapse. It prompted her to again send a letter to Barnet.

"I know that you're very unhappy with me, as I am with myself," Brooks wrote. "I didn't plan it or want to do it. My impulsive behavior took over and I couldn't stop myself. Judge Barnet, please try to understand I did not intentionally relapse."

Her regrets aside, Joni Brooks's dangerous life on the edge, and occasional arrests, would continue until she ran out of time.

On August 24, 1998, Brooks was treated in the emergency room of Ball Memorial Hospital for a broken wrist.

She was reported to be highly intoxicated as a result of cocaine ingestion and would provide few details about how she been injured, other than to say someone had "grabbed" her.

The last contact authorities had with Brooks while she was alive came on November 6, 1998, when she was arrested and booked into the Delaware County jail.

That arrest would not result in the filing of formal charges.

Twelve weeks later, on the late morning of January 29, 1999, a postal carrier driving down Delaware County Road 700-E, just south of Centennial Avenue, noticed what appeared to be the nude, lifeless body of a woman lying facedown in a water-filled ditch, along the west side of the road.

As she drove to a business down the road to ask someone to call authorities, the postal carrier tried to persuade herself that perhaps what she had seen had been a mannequin.

Sadly, that wasn't the case. Because of their repeated dealings with her over the past decade, some of the law enforcement officers called to the scene that day recognized the deceased woman to be Brooks.

Joni Brooks's grave. *Photo by Douglas Walker.*

An autopsy would show that Brooks had drowned in that ditch, where the depth of the water was measured at eight inches.

The amount of cocaine in her system prompted some to speculate that Brooks was likely unconscious at the time she went into the ditch.

Delaware County coroner James St. Myer also reporting finding signs of "blunt force trauma" on the Muncie woman's head, torso, arms and legs.

JANUARY 29, 1999

Local news: Muncie police were attempting to determine how a forty-six-year-old Muncie man's body ended up in a Randolph County landfill. Also, an out-of-county prosecutor dismissed racketeering charges against former Delaware County Democratic Party chairman Phil Nichols and two former county officials.

Music: The top popular song in the United States was "Baby One More Time" by Britney Spears.

TV: *Who Wants to Be a Millionaire*, hosted by television veteran Regis Philbin, dominated TV ratings in January 1999.

Movies: *Varsity Blues*, a "coming-of-age comedy drama," was the nation's top film for two weeks in January 1999.

Books: *A Man in Full* by Tom Wolfe and *The Greatest Generation* by NBC newsman Tom Brokaw topped bestseller lists.

Those injuries hadn't caused her death but suggested she had been handled roughly in her final hours and perhaps had even been thrown down the ditch bank into the water.

"This case sticks in my mind," Bob Pyle, a retired Delaware County sheriff's investigator who led the investigation into Brooks's death, told the *Star Press* in 2013.

"I think it was somebody she knew, somebody she did business with. I hate to say it, but it was a drug relationship or prostitution gone wrong."

There was speculation in the wake of her death that Brooks's last dose of cocaine had caused an overdose, prompting her companions that night to believe she had died and, in a panic, dispose of her body at an isolated location.

Some suggested Brooks could have been targeted because she had been too talkative about an associate's criminal activities.

Investigators spoke to as many as one hundred people who might have known something about Brooks's final hours.

"We still kind of have somebody in the back of our minds," Pyle said fourteen years after her death. "But I don't think it will ever come out. Everybody was scared of him then, and they're scared of him now."

Both Pyle and Nate Jackson, another sheriff's investigator who worked the case and was at the scene this morning Brooks's body was discovered, said it was certainly possible more than one person was responsible for her death or dumping her in the ditch.

"I think there's more than one that knows what happened," Jackson said.

Pyle said he became friends with Brooks's mother, who had been a coworker of his wife.

"When you have a little bit of a personal connection, it stays with you," he said. "But any homicide, you make a connection with the family. You're feeling their pain because you're with them at their worst time ever."

An investigator's file on Joni Brooks's death contained a document, apparently distributed at her funeral, that featured a poem written by the Muncie woman, in the final year of her life, on one side.

On the other side were the lyrics of a song that apparently had a special significance to Brooks—the 1971 Led Zeppelin classic "Stairway to Heaven."

Brooks's tombstone—in a quiet cemetery in northern Henry County, not far from where she grew up—also has the title to that song in an engraving.

The other side of the stone features the names of the children Joni Brooks gave birth to and loved.

If You Have Information

If you have information that could help the investigation into this cold case, contact the Delaware County Sheriff's Office. Sheriff Tony Skinner asks that you go to www.delawarecountysheriff.com and click on the CONTACT tab to find telephone numbers to call as well as a contact form that can be filled out anonymously.

A CIVIL WAR VETERAN'S SLAYING
GOES UNSOLVED

After his brother was murdered on Muncie's south side, John B. Stoll—editor of a South Bend newspaper and a player in state Democratic politics—predicted that "astonishing arrests [will] eventually be made in this case."

Nearly 125 years later, such arrests—astonishing or otherwise—have yet to be made.

The body of William Blocher Stoll, a fifty-three-year-old Civil War veteran who had lived in Muncie for eleven years, was discovered by a pair of men delivering ice to south-side homes shortly after dawn on Sunday, September 4, 1898.

Stoll was found facedown near Seventh Street, about one hundred feet from his family's home in the 1300 block of South Elm Street. He had suffered two head injuries, including a large wound on his left temple that apparently caused his death.

Police determined that Stoll, an employee at the local Gill Brothers pot factory, had spent the previous evening at Harry Webster's saloon, at Ninth and Walnut Streets, drinking several glasses of beer and playing cards.

There had been no reports of trouble at the tavern. The possibility Stoll was the victim of a robbery was also discounted—he was determined to be carrying $1.05 and a gold watch when his body was found.

The proximity of Stoll's body to his home—where he lived with his wife, son, two daughters, a son-in-law and a male boarder—combined with other factors to draw speculation the Muncie man night have been a victim of domestic violence.

The grave of William Stoll. *Photo by Douglas Walker.*

According to the *Muncie Daily Herald*, physicians said it was possible the mortally wounded Stoll had lain on his back for at least an hour before "being turned in the position in which he was found."

A coroner, meanwhile, said it appeared blood had been wiped from the victim's face and hands prior to the body's discovery.

By September 7, however, the *Muncie Morning News* reported the theory "the body was carried where it was found after the assault at some other place has been discarded, and the belief is the man was struck dead in his tracks and kicked from the sidewalk by the murderer."

Bright moonlight the night of the killing would have made transporting the body "very dangerous," the article said.

On September 6, the victim's widow, Ardelia, issued a statement: "I will pay a reward of $50 for any information that will lead to the arrest and conviction of the murderer or murderers of my husband on the night of Sept. 4."

The money—which Mrs. Stoll had "earned by work washing clothes and cooking for boarders"—was given to Muncie's British-born police superintendent, Samuel B. Cashmore, for safekeeping.

The *Morning News* reported the reward had been offered in part to "remove the stain of suspicion" from the family.

Three witnesses—including the boarder sleeping inside the Stoll house, and the victim's twenty-two-year-old son, Harry, who spent the night outside sleeping in a hammock—said they had briefly heard an apparent disagreement, with shouting, in the distance about midnight on the evening of the slaying.

On September 7, the *Indianapolis Journal* reported Prosecutor Henry L. Hopping had, after interviews, "expressed a belief that no member of the family was connected to the crime."

The *Indianapolis News*, however, later denied the family had been exonerated.

The unsolved killing drew coverage from newspapers in other areas of Indiana, particularly in the northern part of the state, likely due to the victim's brother, John, and his notoriety as a South Bend newspaper editor.

One article called William Stoll a "peaceable, inoffensive and unassuming and unpretentious citizen" who was "not known to have any enemies in the town."

Eventually, investigators determined there was, perhaps, one potential enemy of William Stoll, and that man had also been in Webster's saloon on the evening of September 3.

Cyrus Wilkinson several years earlier had been a boarder at the Stoll home until William Stoll had "compelled him to leave" for having "too intimate a relationship" with one of Stoll's daughters.

Wilkinson maintained there were no lasting hard feelings and said William Stoll had greeted him amiably at the tavern, offering to buy him a drink, an offer Wilkinson said he declined.

He also said he had no contact with Stoll after leaving the tavern. Wilkinson maintained he had gone home, although he said he had slept "in the hay mow in his barn" rather than joining his wife in their house.

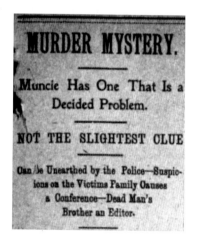

MURDER MYSTERY.

Muncie Has One That Is a Decided Problem.

NOT THE SLIGHTEST CLUE

Can be Unearthed by the Police—Suspicions on the Victims Family Causes a Conference—Dead Man's Brother an Editor.

A newspaper headline from the time of William Stoll's killing. *From the authors' collection.*

SEPTEMBER 4, 1898

Local news: In September 1898, a twenty-nine-year-old Muncie woman attempted suicide when police arrived at her home to arrest her, swallowing "enough morphine to have killed a dozen persons." She was saved with the use of a stomach pump. The woman's eighty-year-old husband had reported she was nearly starving him, spending his limited income on "morphine, whisky, snuff and tobacco."

Books: Popular books published in 1898 included *War of the Worlds* by H.G. Wells and *Caesar and Cleopatra* by George Bernard Shaw.

On the evening of Monday, September 12—eight days after the slaying—Wilkinson was taken into custody by Muncie police.

While the *Daily Herald* reported on September 13 that Wilkinson had told "numerous conflicting and contradictory stories," he was released from custody that day. Police superintendent Cashmore acknowledged there was no evidence on which charges could be filed.

Wilkinson's brief detention marked the only time anyone would be jailed as a result of William Stoll's death.

On April 28, 1900, Cyrus Wilkinson, by then living on a property about two miles west of Muncie, swallowed two ounces of carbolic acid and ten minutes later died "in terrific agony."

A *Muncie Morning Star* article blamed the suicide on "ill health and business troubles," reporting the forty-three-year-old Wilkinson was on the verge of losing his farm.

More than a century after his great-great-grandfather's slaying, Muncie resident Richard Stahl (the family had long since changed the spelling of their surname) learned about the unsolved murder through the genealogy research of his wife, Stephanie.

Stahl has studied the surviving materials related to the homicide and said there appears to be reason to consider both of the main theories—that William Stoll was attacked by one or more members of his household or was the victim of former tenant Cyrus Wilkinson.

He has also researched his ancestor's service in the Civil War, visiting the site of the Battle of Fredericksburg, Virginia, where William Stoll—serving in a Pennsylvania infantry unit—was wounded in December 1862.

Through the efforts of his great-great-grandson, William Stoll's long-unmarked grave in Muncie's Beech Grove Cemetery now has a marker noting his Civil War service.

"I was glad to get that for him," Richard Stahl said.

HOLIDAY HOMICIDE

Ruby Dean Moore never had a chance.

In the week before Christmas 1964, when someone decided to end Moore's life—and it was an at-times troubled life, based on surviving documentation—the thirty-six-year-old Muncie woman likely was unable to do much to defend herself.

That's because, a postmortem examination would show, her blood-alcohol content measured at 0.40, five times the legal limit for Indiana motorists under 2023 standards.

An autopsy would determine Moore had been beaten to death, although pathologists said the victim's high BAC could have been a contributing factor.

Moore's remains were found on December 24, on what was recalled as a rainy Thursday morning, by rural Chesterfield resident John LeMond and his nine-year-old son, Kirby, as they hunted near the High Banks Bridge, carrying Delaware County Road 300-S over the White River.

Delaware County sheriff's deputies, along with state troopers and officers from nearby Yorktown, were called to the scene.

The body was facedown in a pile of leaves east of the river and 256 feet north of the county road, on farmland owned by Ed Orebaugh.

The victim, clad in red pants and a blue corduroy jacket, was fully clothed, with the exception of her missing left shoe.

It was immediately apparent that the woman had been a victim of violence. Her left eye, and the left side of her face, were severely swollen.

The bridge near where Ruby Dean Moore's body was found. *Photo by Keith Roysdon.*

Delaware County coroner Galion Stephens would identify the victim as Ruby Dean Wallace Moore, most recently a resident of the 2000 block of East Dartmouth Avenue in Muncie's Morningside neighborhood.

According to an autopsy report—not filed until August 1966 by Bryan Pitman, Stephens's successor as county coroner—Moore had suffered a ruptured liver due to "abdominal trauma," likely caused by a blow from a "blunt instrument, such as the human hand and fist."

In 1965, Russell Fisher, at the time chief medical examiner for the state of Maryland, was asked to review forensic evidence in the Moore case, and concluded the victim likely died less than an hour after suffering the liver injury.

After the body was identified, the victim's husband, Charles "Sam" Moore, was contacted in Hartford City, where the brickmason was at work on a project. The couple's two young children were in the care of a babysitter.

Family members said they hadn't seen Ruby Moore for several days.

It wasn't the first time she had disappeared. In January 1960, Charles Moore reported his wife missing after she had failed to return home for nine days.

"The missing woman was believed possibly to have gone to Ohio," the *Muncie Evening Press* reported at that time. Her eventual return to Muncie did not result in a follow-up article.

Those investigating Moore's death at first believed she had been killed two or three days before her body was discovered.

On December 26, however, three Anderson men—who had read media accounts about the killing—told deputies they had been hunting in the same area on December 19 when they found what was later determined to be Moore's missing shoe, about 225 feet from where her body was discovered five days later.

Noting that the shoes were not muddy, investigators suggested Moore's body had been carried to the location where it was found.

Within hours of the body's discovery, authorities told the *Muncie Star* they had "strong leads" in the case.

Two days after that, Delaware County sheriff Harry Howard said several people who had been with Moore in her last days had been questioned.

On the evening of December 28, deputies accompanied a Muncie man, whose name was not revealed to reporters, to Indianapolis, where he voluntarily submitted to a lie detector test.

The following day, investigators said they were submitting evidence in the case, not described to the media, to be examined by FBI officials in Washington, D.C.

In spite of the claims of "strong leads," the investigation of Moore's slaying appears to have quickly stalled. No related arrest was ever made.

"We know the identity of the person we want, but as yet, we are unable to prove our case in court," Sheriff Howard told the *Evening Press* in February 1966. "The case is under active investigation."

Nearly five decades later, in December 2013, investigators with the sheriff's office told the *Star Press* they could find no file on the unsolved 1964 homicide.

Also at that time, two of Moore's survivors declined to discuss her life or death.

The Moore case was also one that quickly faded in terms of local media coverage, perhaps in part due to its timing, with the body being discovered on Christmas Eve.

Another slaying, three days after Moore's body was found, drew considerably more attention. It involved a man fatally shooting his estranged wife in Muncie amid allegations of bigamy.

Records provide only scant details about Ruby Moore and her life, in Muncie or elsewhere.

DECEMBER 24, 1964

Local news: A dispute had developed over whether the marching bands from Ball State and Indiana State colleges would be able to participate in the January 20 parade in Washington, D.C., commemorating President Lyndon B. Johnson's inauguration. Invitations had been extended to both bands, but an official later referred to the invites as "iffy."

Music: "I Feel Fine" became the sixth No. 1 single of the year for The Beatles.

TV: *Bonanza* was the nation's top-rated TV series, followed by *Bewitched* and *Gomer Pyle USMC*. The stop-motion animated special *Rudolph the Red-Nosed Reindeer* premiered on NBC-TV.

Movies: The James Bond film *Goldfinger* opened in U.S. theaters.

Books: *Herzog* by Saul Bellow was at the top of bestseller lists.

She was born in Kentucky in May 1928 and apparently moved with her family to Delaware County in 1940.

By the early 1950s, she was married to Moore, a World War II veteran. Court records reflect one or both of the Moores filed for divorce repeatedly during that decade. At least once, a divorce was granted and Charles Moore received custody of the couple's children.

The couple reconciled, however. In September 1963, their third child, Donna Jean, apparently died at birth.

The 1950s also saw Ruby Moore first arrested for public intoxication. It would happen repeatedly for the remainder of her life. At the time of her death, newspapers reported she had been convicted of the misdemeanor five times in 1963 alone.

Moore was most often employed as a cook or waitress at Muncie restaurants, including the downtown Colonial Café and the Checkerboard House on Burlington Drive. Her final job was at a restaurant in the downtown ABC Bus Station.

On December 28, 1964, Ruby Dean Moore was laid to rest in Elm Ridge Cemetery, not far from where her father, Calvin Morris Wallace, was buried in 1961, and her baby daughter Donna Jean had been buried a little more than a year earlier.

Nearly two decades after her killing, a tombstone was placed on Ruby Moore's grave.

If You Have Information

If you have information that could help the investigation into this cold case, contact the Delaware County Sheriff's Office. Sheriff Tony Skinner asks that you go to www.delawarecountysheriff.com and click on the CONTACT tab to find telephone numbers to call as well as a contact form that can be filled out anonymously.

A NEED TO SEE JUSTICE DONE
IN HIS SON'S MURDER

alletano Cisneros is blunt and straightforward in talking about his past during an interview about the murder of his son, Sebastian Cisneros.

The seventy-five-year-old Texas resident noted that he's lived in the small city of Cuero, Texas, most of his life.

"I lived here except for a little stint in Texas DOC (Department of Correction) when I was seventeen," Calletano Cisneros said. "I was convicted on a murder charge and served ten years before I got the governor's pardon."

"I was seventeen and drunk in a bar and killed this gentleman," he added. "In prison, I stayed out of trouble and people wrote letters to the governor on my behalf and I was twenty-seven years old when I got out."

That experience informs why he wants to see someone arrested and prosecuted for the April 2009 murder of his son, who was thirty-three years old when he was shot to death outside his south-side Muncie home.

"I did my time," he said. "I'd like to see the same justice done in my son's case."

After midnight in the early-morning hours of April 23, 2009, Muncie police were called to Sebastian Cisneros's home in the 1400 block of Ribble Avenue. Neighbors had told police they heard gunshots.

The first officer on the scene found the man later identified as Cisneros on the ground next to the street. He "took a few short breaths" before he stopped breathing, according to a police report.

Cisneros had been shot twice in the chest and once lower in the abdomen.

Right: Sebastian Cisneros. *Provided by Calletano Cisneros.*

Below: The house where Sebastian Cisneros was killed. *Photo by Keith Roysdon.*

He was taken by ambulance to the emergency department at Ball Memorial Hospital but could not be resuscitated.

His house had been ransacked.

Neighbors said a woman in a white Cadillac had dropped Cisneros off not long before he was shot. After shots had rung out, a man dressed in dark clothing was seen running down the street, disappearing into a house or between houses. A .357-caliber handgun used to kill Cisneros was found in a yard a few blocks away.

For a 2011 cold case article by the authors of this book, police investigators said they heard "dozens" of scenarios about Cisneros's killing. One of the theories is that Cisneros interrupted someone who was searching his home.

Police said it was possible that his killer or killers broke into the house because they believed Cisneros was selling marijuana. He had, in 2003, pleaded guilty to possession of marijuana and other charges and was sentenced to a year in jail in Henry County. He had previously been convicted of delivery of marijuana in DeWitt County, Texas, in 1995. He lived in Henry County for a while after his stint in jail there and later moved to Muncie.

He didn't find Muncie better for his fortunes.

Sebastian Cisneros had worked for pipeline and energy companies in Texas and Indiana. His obituary noted that he enjoyed grilling and spending time with his children, two sons and a daughter.

He had grown up in Cuero, which his father noted in an interview was "at one time the turkey capital of the world."

Calletano said his son was "a nice kid" but "kind of hard-headed."

"I was always going to the principal's office when he got in trouble. Before I knew it, he got into trouble…for selling dope, selling marijuana to this guy.

"My late wife died, and he was kind of own his own. I had a bunch of [guys] living with me. I told Sebastian these guys were helping me pay the bills. But he was wild and drinking, and he beat up one of the guys staying with me.

"He left Cuero and ended up in New Castle," Calletano said. "He came back to Cuero with a new wife, then went back to New Castle."

Less than a month before he was shot to death, Cisneros called Muncie police at about 3:00 a.m. to report two women had broken a window in an attempt to enter his house. A week before he was killed, he again called police to say that a woman he knew had stolen his pickup truck.

Police couldn't prove any connection between Cisneros's trouble with one woman in particular and his death.

"One morning I'm eating cereal and somebody called and they said, 'I'm the coroner from Muncie.' He asked if I was Sebastian's dad: 'He was killed last night.'

"That tore me up.

"My daughter said, let's go to Indiana. I talked to the police department and they had some names of individuals, they gave me the names of four or five people from Cuero they had seen in Muncie.

APRIL 23, 2009

Local news: An Indianapolis labor and election attorney acknowledged that labor unions had paid his legal fees for his work on behalf of Jim Mansfield, the Democratic Party candidate challenging Republican Sharon McShurley in the mayoral campaign.

Music: The *Billboard* top hit single on April 23, 2009, was "Boom Boom Pow" by the Black Eyed Peas.

Movies: The top movie at the box office for the date was Disney's *Earth*, followed by *17 Again* and *State of Play*.

TV: The top-rated television shows on April 23, 2009, were *60 Minutes*, followed by *Who Wants to Be a Millionaire?*

Books: *Long Lost*, by Harlan Coben, was the top *New York Times* bestseller for the week leading up to April 23, 2009.

"I don't know if those guys had anything to do with it."

At some point, Calletano said, he received a call from someone at U.S. Homeland Security.

"He said he was going to look into it, but I never heard back from them."

Sebastian Cisneros's murder came at a busy period of homicides in Muncie.

In May 2009, the *Star Press* newspaper reported that, after investigating one homicide in the previous two calendar years, Muncie police found themselves investigating four in a nine-week period.

James Danson "J.D." Edwards was shot to death a little more than a month after Cisneros was killed. In March, Jennifer Stafford had been beaten to death in her east-side mobile home and nineteen-year-old Tameka Huff had been shot to death.

It was a period that, for number of deaths if not the unsolved status of the majority of the cases, rivals the "murder season" of 1979 as documented in another chapter in this book. Police noted, however, that the four slayings in the spring of 2009 were committed under "vastly different" circumstances and arrests had been made in three of the four. Only Cisneros's killing had not resulted in an arrest and, as of 2023, still had not.

Calletano urged the *Star Press* newspaper in Muncie to continue to report on his son's murder.

"I looked up Muncie and it said it had something to do with the KKK and I thought, 'Muncie's not going to do anything.' He was Mexican-American and a drug addict.

"I just gave up hope."

He said he hopes having his son's story retold in this book might prompt some new information.

"I just want some justice," he said.

If You Have Information

If you have information that could help an investigation into this cold case, contact the Muncie Police Department. Police chief Nate Sloan asks that you contact the Criminal Investigations Division of the Muncie Police Department at 765-747-4867.

"I DREAM I SEE BLOOD"

The thought has been going through Christy Pinnick's mind for nearly thirty years: Not long before her father was killed, she saw the men she believes killed him.

Christy, the daughter of Raymond "Sandy" Pinnick, was twenty years old and working the cash register at Rite-Aid drugs on the evening of February 11, 1994, when three men came into the store; picked up a few things, including bottles of liquor; and checked out at her register.

Christy knew at least a couple of the men. She knew they were acquaintances of her father, who at forty-one had some brushes with the law in his past. But Ray Pinnick had worked at Indiana Ticket for more than twenty years and was working hard at the job.

That night, at that now-long-gone Muncie pharmacy across a parking lot from a now-long-gone Kmart, Christy recognized one of the men as someone who knew her father.

"Dad didn't like [him] and he didn't want him around the house," she recalled in an interview. "He said [the man] was a narc," or someone who was an informant for the police.

When the men came to her register, "I remember saying hello, and that's about all I remember," she said.

Christy finished her drugstore shift at 9:00 p.m. and stopped at her mother's house to borrow a blender: A friend was going to stay overnight, and "we were going to make margaritas."

Christy Pinnick holding a family photo. *Photo by Keith Roysdon.*

She left her mom's house, picked up her nearly-three-year-old son, Calvin, from the babysitter and headed home to the house she shared with her dad on Purdue Avenue in Muncie's Morningside neighborhood.

She found her father in a pool of blood on the floor of their kitchen, just inside the back door.

In the nearly thirty years since, Christy has been told by many people that the three men she saw in the drugstore that night killed her father. She knows their names and rattles them off in quick succession when asked.

No one has been arrested and charged with Ray Pinnick's murder. She's pushed police to investigate and charge her father's killers, to the point she thinks police no longer want to hear from her.

Time has not tempered Christy's desire that justice be done.

"I have nightmares," she said. "I dream I see blood."

Christy's mom and dad divorced when she was young. She lived with her dad, and her younger brother, Chris, lived with their mother.

Pictures of the Pinnicks show a happy American family. Ray Pinnick is always smiling in the pictures. In one of the snapshots, he's wearing an umbrella hat and smiling at someone to his left, just outside the photo.

Raymond Pinnick. *Photo provided by family.*

Ray and Christy Pinnick. *Photo provided by family.*

Ray loved to cook and have company over, and his daughter remembers him as good-natured and easygoing.

He sometimes made a little extra money, besides his pay from Indiana Ticket, by selling marijuana, and Christy acknowledges that some people might think that meant her father was "no angel."

In an interview a few years ago for a cold case newspaper article by the authors, she said she couldn't understand why someone would want to kill her father. She didn't know him to have any enemies, she said.

But in the years following his murder, Christy began to believe three men did indeed want to kill her father—or at least were willing to do so.

"He was lying on the floor," Christy recalled in a 2022 interview for this book.

She's sitting outside, in the shade, on this sunny day. By her feet is a canvas bag of zucchini, tomatoes and other vegetables she brought to give to the interviewer. In her lap is a framed family photo.

The warm, bright day contrasts with her memories of the dark night in February 1994 when she came home and found her father's body.

"I came in the back door, and he was lying in a pool of blood," she remembers.

Christy put young Calvin in a large closet nearby so he wouldn't see his grandfather.

Christy thought her father had fallen and hit his head on a nearby tank that had been, until a few days before, home to Goliath, her father's pet python. The snake had escaped not long before but was found in the house a few days after her father's death.

"I didn't realize he had been murdered," she said. "I thought that Dad had slipped and had hit his head on (the snake's) tank." She paused and repeated, "I thought he slipped and fell and hit his head."

Within a few hours that night, Christy Pinnick found out her father had been murdered. The realization came only after she had been taken to Muncie police offices, her fingerprints had been taken and an investigator asked who she thought did it.

"They told me it was being treated as a homicide," she said.

The autopsy examination, conducted under the supervision of then–Delaware County coroner Jack Stonebraker Jr., showed that Ray Pinnick died from a single gunshot wound to the head.

Stonebraker's 1994 coroner's report indicated the motive for Pinnick's murder was not robbery: investigators found $1,104 in cash in the back pockets of his jeans, and there were drugs in the house. Neither the cash nor the drugs were taken.

Ray Pinnick was shot near the right ear and fell into the aquarium where Goliath had lived, shattering the glass and creating a scene that had led Christy to believe her father had simply fallen into the aquarium.

After the authors of this book quoted Christy Pinnnick in a December 2012 newspaper article about her father's unsolved murder, she says she got a call from the police. But it wasn't with news about a break in the case.

"Why did you go to the newspaper and not us?" she said the police investigator asked her. "They were pretty ticked at me. 'Why didn't you talk to us?' and I said, 'I talked to you for twenty years, and it didn't do any good.'"

Christy Pinnick's dealings with the police have never been easy.

"The night my dad was killed, a policeman told me my dad deserved what he got," she said. "I'll never forget that."

Not long after that night, people told her they believed the three men who had come into her store, the men who knew him, had killed her father.

"Store security gave me tapes of the three of them when they were there," she said. "I tried giving them to the police, and they told me they had no way of running them." The tapes were later destroyed when a basement where Christy had stored them was flooded.

Over the years, Christy has pursued her own investigation of her father's murder. She found herself going over everything she heard and everything she knew.

"A week before, I remember hearing my dad arguing with someone." Her father later talked about wanting to move out of Muncie.

In the weeks and months that followed, she kept hearing people mention the names of the three men. Friends said they heard that the men had killed her father.

FEBRUARY 11, 1994

Local news: Felix Rippy, an attorney running against incumbent Richard Reed for Delaware County prosecutor, said he received a card calling into question his claim that he lived in Delaware County. The card was received at his apartment in Hamilton County. The return address on the piece of mail, a thank-you card, was for a post office box for Reed's campaign. Muncie Community Schools superintendent Sam Abram announced he was leaving the school system for a position with schools in Pontiac, Michigan. The first annual report for employee-owned Indiana Steel & Wire was optimistic.

Music: The top songs on the *Billboard* Hot 100 included "All for Love" by Bryan Adams, Rod Stewart and Sting; "Hero" by Mariah Carey; and "The Power of Love," by Celine Dion.

Movies: The top movie was *Ace Ventura: Pet Detective*, released on February 4, 1994.

TV: Bill Cosby had just returned to TV in *The Cosby Mysteries*, airing on January 31.

Books: *Disclosure* by Michael Crichton was at the top of the *New York Times* bestseller list from mid-January to mid-February.

"They always say these names," she said.

Citing one of the men by name, she added, "They said he's bad news, stay away from him."

While she was going around Muncie, asking people what they knew about her father's murder, Christy heard something else.

"The word got back to me if I didn't back off, they would get to me through my son."

When Christy Pinnick sat down to talk about her father's death in 2022, the passage of time came up.

"It's been twenty-eight years," she said. "My son is thirty-two."

She said she "went the wrong direction for a couple of years" after her father's murder, but then she turned her life around.

"I took my butt to school and became a medical assistant," she said. She works for a medical company that provides services to school employees.

One of the three men she believes killed her father has died. A few times, she's seen the man she believes most responsible for her father's death, the man her father warned was a police informant and who others said was "bad news," around town.

That night, the night she found her father, is still vivid in her mind, and she knows what she hopes happens.

"I would like to see them pay for what they did, for taking my dad's life. I know they have family too and it's going to hurt their families too. But I'd like to see them pay for what they did.

"More than anything, I'd like to know why."

IF YOU HAVE INFORMATION

If you have information that could help an investigation into this cold case, contact the Muncie Police Department. Police chief Nate Sloan asks that you contact the Criminal Investigations Division of the Muncie Police Department at 765-747-4867.

RUNNING WITH SOME BAD PEOPLE

The date of death on Howard "Pete" Journay's headstone reads only "April 1979." That's because there's uncertainty over exactly when he died.

What's not uncertain is how Journay died: Beaten to death and thrown into the Mississinewa River in northern Delaware County. His body was recovered from the river on May 8, 1979.

Before his remains were buried in Beech Grove Cemetery in Muncie, before his body was found in the river, Journay lived an uncertain and perhaps lonely life. Investigators looking into his death got little help determining the names of friends of associates: Journay had been estranged from his family because of his substance abuse.

Journay was remembered by police for his rowdy presence at local bars and taverns after he'd been drinking.

How much his lifestyle played into his death is, like a lot of things about Pete Journay, uncertain.

When he died in April 1979, Journay was thirty-seven years old. He'd attended local schools and worked in a few jobs around town, but he was perhaps best known as a man who liked to party.

"Pete was into alcohol and liked to fight a lot," Jerry Cook, a longtime Delaware County sheriff's deputy and investigator, said for a December 2012 article about Journay by the authors of this book.

"He was rowdy."

The Mississinewa River near where Pete Journay's body was found. *Photo by Keith Roysdon.*

Two men from Hartford City, in Blackford County north of Muncie, were fishing at a bridge over the Mississinewa River, just north of the town of Wheeling, when they saw a body in the water. They called police.

The body was treated as a John Doe early in the investigation. The remains carried no identification and had decomposed. But the tattoo of a snake wrapped around a dagger on the upper arm was distinctive.

An article appeared in the newspaper calling for help in identifying the body. Journay's sister, Nancy, contacted police and said her brother hadn't been seen since April 28. And ultimately police were able to match fingerprints from the body to those taken when Journay had been arrested before.

Cook remembered the discovery of Journay's body and subsequent investigation.

"The water was clear and you could see his body," Cook recalled in a 2022 interview for this book.

After the discovery had been made, the investigation itself was murkier.

"I was one of the divers that went into that river," Cook said. "We dove looking for a gun but never found it."

By May, newspaper accounts indicated that police believed Journay's body had been thrown over the side of the nearby bridge and that his body initially settled into a pool in a deeper portion of the river. But the body eventually surfaced.

Coroner Larry Cole said he believed Journay had been struck in the head as many as twenty times.

Journay was last seen at Gene's Tavern, a South Walnut Street bar, at about 1:00 a.m. on April 29. Two women at the bar that night—Arlene R. Larson and her daughter, Tina A. Grueshow—were working as waitresses and were believed to be the last to see Journay alive. The two were later arrested and convicted on charges related to the spring 1979 death of James W. "Jay" Buffin. Police said in May 1979 that the two women were not suspects in Journay's death.

Later in his life, according to a police report, Journay's family saw less and less of him. "It seems that generally about the only time he came around was when he had been drinking and then he caused problems," according to the police report.

Police knew Journay but weren't harshly critical of him in the 2012 article.

"Pete had been around for a while," veteran county police investigator Jerry Golden recalled. "He was never real bad. He was one of those guys that always seemed to be around someplace. He ran with some people that had been in trouble with the law."

Among those people were those connected to another 1979 murder, that of Paula Garrett, the subject of another chapter in this book. Like Journay, Garrett was killed by numerous blows to the head with a blunt object.

"If I remember, Pete had some association with some people involved in that one," Golden said in 2012. "He had some association with it. They wondered if it was connected. They never established a connection that I know of."

Back in 2012, for the article about Journay's death, veteran county police sergeant Gregg Ellison voiced the hope that every investigator feels regarding cold cases.

"It's not unthinkable it could be resolved," Ellison said. "People's consciences work on them that long and they may come forward. It happens that cases that are old are actually solved."

Journay's funeral service was held on May 12, 1979, in a private gathering at Meeks Mortuary. There were no calling hours for visitors, and no survivors were named in the obituary that appeared in that morning's paper. An obituary the day before had listed four children and three sisters as survivors. The obituaries noted that he was born in Muncie and attended Lincoln

MAY 8, 1979

Local news: The number of people working in Muncie was 56,300, up by 3,500 from February/March, the local unemployment office announced. Unemployment was 6.7 percent. Passenger train service through Amtrak changed times slightly. The daily train to Chicago left at 9:55 a.m.

Music: "Reunited" by Peaches and Herb.

Movies: The top movie was *Last Embrace*, starring Roy Scheider.

TV: The top-rated TV series was *Mork & Mindy*, followed by the miniseries *Ike* and then *Three's Company* and *Laverne & Shirley*.

Books: The *New York Times* top bestseller from April 29 through July 15, 1979, was *The Matarese Circle* by Robert Ludlum.

Elementary School, Wilson Junior High and Central High School and that he worked for a landscaping company.

Pete Journay wasn't forgotten by those who loved him. Back in the days when people took out "In Memoriam" ads in the classified sections of newspapers, Journay's passing was marked in one of those ads, appearing on page 15 of the *Muncie Evening Press* on April 29, 1980, a year after his death.

"In loving memory of Howard Pete Journay, who passed away April 1980. Sadly missed by Nancy & Family."

Unfortunately, the ad got the year of his death wrong.

IF YOU HAVE INFORMATION

If you have information that could help the investigation into this cold case, contact the Delaware County Sheriff's Office. Sheriff Tony Skinner asks that you go to www.delawarecountysheriff.com and click on the CONTACT tab to find telephone numbers to call as well as a contact form that can be filled out anonymously.

THE MURDER SEASON OF 1979

In March 1979, Muncie was riding high. The beloved Muncie Central Bearcats had just won their seventh state high school boys basketball championship. Bearcats fans immediately began a chant: "Eight in '80!"

The U.S. Census would soon show the city's population at 76,460, a 10 percent increase over the decade of the 1970s and likely the high point for the city. Local school enrollment was high. The workforce was strong at manufacturing plants like Warner Gear and Chevrolet Muncie.

Department stores like JCPenney anchored Muncie Mall, which was approaching its tenth year as a shopping center for the city. Muncie still had two Kmart stores, on the north and south sides. Moviegoers could see their new films at their choice of venues: the Delaware Cinema, Northwest Plaza Cinema, the Rivoli, Movies at Muncie Mall or the Muncie and Ski-Hi drive-ins.

And a killer, or killers, were at work.

Three killings kept police investigators busy from March to May 1979 and for weeks and months beyond.

Two of these three crimes remain unsolved, and those two, the March 25 killing of Paula Garrett and the May 8 killing of Howard "Pete" Journay, are detailed in other chapters of this book because of their status as cold cases. The May 20 killing of James "Jay" Buffin was successfully prosecuted.

In the minds of some professional and amateur investigators, all three murders were linked.

By any measure, the spring of 1979 was a particularly bloody one in Muncie and Delaware County.

Certainly, the community had seen homicide-intensive periods before. In *The Westside Park Murders*, the true crime book by the authors of this volume and published by The History Press in 2021, officials looked back on the late 1970s and early 1980s, which then–Delaware County prosecutor Richard Reed cited as a period of "one homicide after another."

The three murders in the spring of 1979 came in such rapid succession the period looks, in retrospect, especially brutal.

"There was a lot going on," said Jerry Cook, a longtime county police investigator who later served as a prosecutor's office investigator.

Veteran police officers recalled the period for a Cold Case Muncie article in the *Star Press* newspaper by the authors of this book:

"Jerry Golden, a retired county police investigator who also spent years in the prosecutor's office, agreed that 'there was a lot going on at that time' and much of it was happening on the city's south side," the article noted.

"'At one time, that end of town was pretty rough,' Golden said. 'It was rougher than it is now.'"

Investigators very quickly connected the sixty-year-old Buffin's death to Journay's killing. Within hours after Buffin's body was found by a neighbor, and police determined the man had been stabbed to death, warrants were issued for people who frequented a south-side Muncie bar. Four of them lived in the house where Buffin's body was found.

Two of those persons were among the last to have seen Journay alive before he disappeared and was later found dead.

In the Buffin investigation, two people were found guilty of involuntary manslaughter and voluntary manslaughter, respectively. Neither of the defendants was sentenced to more than ten years in prison.

Paula Garrett's son, Eric, wrote a book about his mother's death. *Unprosecuted* was published in 2020, and in it, Eric Garrett made connections between the murder of his mother and the still-unsolved murder of Howard "Pete" Journay.

Eric Garrett, who believes that a man who had dated his mother killed her and assaulted him that night in 1979, quoted people who knew his mother as saying that Journay was with his mother's killer the night she was killed.

The book says that Journay, who had been waiting in the alleged killer's pickup truck, came inside and saw the bloody aftermath of Paula Garrett's slaying.

The killer threatened Journay and told him to keep his mouth shut, Eric Garrett says.

Not long after, Journay was in a bar and was telling people there what he had seen.

"Well, of course, Pete was in a bar not long afterward, had a few drinks and starts shooting his mouth off," according to Eric Garrett's book. "About how he was there, saw the blood everywhere."

Someone in the bar made a phone call.

"So now the phone rings at the bar. It's for Pete. He takes the call, then says, 'I'll be right back. There's someone I'm supposed to meet across the street.' They found [him] in the river three days later."

Journay's body was found in the Mississinewa River, as recounted elsewhere in this book.

The spring of 1979 was a bloody time in Delaware County, but the killings related to the victims in those murders didn't stop. Two more generations of the Buffin family saw violent tragedy.

In addition to the 1979 killing of James "Jay" Buffin, in 1985, Gary J. Buffin was shot to death in a pool hall in the town of Selma, east of Muncie. In 1996, the killers of Gary Buffin, son of James "Jay" Buffin and father of Gary J. Buffin, were sentenced to prison for his killing.

The murder season of spring 1979 was not unnoticed, even several years later. In an April 13, 1986 article in the *Muncie Star* newspaper, Diana Newlin wrote, months after the Westside Park slayings of Kimberly Dowell and Ethan Dixon, about some of the outstanding, unsolved murders in recent decades. Some of these cold cases are recounted in this book.

The number of homicides in Delaware County in 1979 were part of a larger trend of a high homicide rate in all of Indiana around that time.

Indiana had a homicide rate of 8.3 per 100,000 population, according to statistics kept by the Federal Bureau of Investigation. That's compared to more than 10 per 100,000 for the entire United States. Indiana ranked twelfth among all fifty states and the District of Columbia for homicides.

That number fell dramatically over the next several years to stand at about 5.0 per 100,000 in the mid-1980s, when it began to increase again, reaching a high of 8.2 per 100,000 in 1992.

Indiana's rate has not been as high as that 8.3 per 100,000 since 1979.

COLD CASE FARM

When Gretchen Binney and her family moved into a rambling house on about ten acres along a rural road in northern Delaware County, they knew a little bit of the one-hundred-year-old property's history.

"We knew that there had been a murder," Binney said. "Our realtor told us even though she didn't have to."

What they didn't know at first was that at least three people had died violent deaths on the property, including a man who hanged himself in the barn and another who shot himself while he sat in his truck.

But the best-known death that took place at the farm along Black Cemetery Road was that of Charles Frank Graham, who was forty-three when he was shot to death on a side porch of his house on August 24, 1988.

It's unclear if Graham heard his assailant coming. When crime scene photos were taken, a cigar was still clenched in one corner of his mouth. He didn't have time to take the cigar out before he was shot twice in the back of the head.

Police quickly determined that Graham wasn't killed because of a robbery or burglary gone bad. That was reported in the first newspaper article about the killing. His wife, Karen, discovered his body at about 11:30 p.m. She was afraid the killer might still be close by, so she went to a neighbor's house and, finding no one home, drove to the Albany Police Department.

Police fairly quickly started getting tips about the killing.

"We've got some good things to follow," Delaware County police chief deputy sheriff Larry Brandon told the *Muncie Evening Press* after the murder. "We're not at a dead end by any means."

The barn on the farm where Charles Frank Graham was killed. *Photo by Keith Roysdon.*

Brandon acknowledged, though, that there was little physical evidence at the scene, which gave investigators little to work with.

At the same time, county police were investigating the death of Donald W. Phillips. Police said Phillips's death was believed to be drug related. Phillips's badly decomposed body had been found in August in a pickup truck along Butterfield Road on the east side of Muncie.

The killings of Graham and Phillips were among eight investigated by local police in 1988.

When the *Muncie Evening Press* recapped the Graham case in a 1990 article, county police investigator Jerry Cook said that so far, investigators had only been able to eliminate leads.

In a 2022 interview for this book, Cook said that over the years, police had heard the killing could be attributed to a dispute over a proposed land purchase: Someone wanted to buy some of Graham's land, but he didn't want to sell.

Black Cemetery Road—which is named for Black Cemetery, not far away from the Graham murder scene—has been the scene of violence and crime a few times over the years.

In 2005, Simon Rios, from Allen County, murdered his wife and their three daughters in their home. In Delaware County, he raped and killed a ten-year-old girl he abducted from a school bus stop in Albany. He confessed and told police where they could find her body, in a wooded area near a gravel pit off Black Cemetery Road.

Charles Graham. *From the authors' collection.*

In 2008, when Rios was found dead, hanging in his cell at the Pendleton Correctional Correction Complex, local law enforcement treated the suicide as good news.

Binney, the current co-owner of the farm along Black Cemetery Road when Graham was killed, said she's heard a few other stories over the years.

She heard from a political candidate whose grandfather shot himself in a pickup truck at some point in the past.

"And the guy who hung himself in the barn, we were told by a neighbor supposedly that happened in the 1970s," she added.

What goes through her mind when she hears stories like that?

"Well, it's an old farm," she said. "It's been here for a hundred years, so people have died here.

"One of our neighbors told us the property was cursed. It's just weird. It made the property cheaper."

Binney said her neighbors believe Graham's killing was a particular kind of slaying.

"Our neighbors believe it was a hit," she said.

Binney, who grew up in a rural area and then lived in Muncie before moving to Black Cemetery Road, said there's an unwritten rule of living in the country.

"It's different in the country," she said. "The rule around here is that if you have trouble, if you're stopped by the side of the road, they're nice enough. But you don't ask questions."

Binney said the farm gives some people the "heebie jeebies."

"Some guys who've done work here say they've seen floating things in the house.

"The barn feels weird," she added. "People who say they're empathic say there's somebody angry there.

"Sometimes in the barn, I feel something. We've had horses in the barn and they don't get spooked and cats will walk right through the barn. But a friend who tells us the place is cursed will stay in his car in the driveway."

An autopsy found that Graham's assailant was close enough to him to leave gunpowder residue in his hair. Three one-hundred-dollar bills and his credit cards remained in his pockets, making robbery an unlikely motive.

The porch where Charles Frank Graham was killed. *Photo by Keith Roysdon.*

AUGUST 24, 1988

Local news: Mayor James P. Carey and two members of Muncie City Council endorsed a plan to finance the construction of a new city hall building. Police identified the victim of a fatal shooting as Donald W. Phillips, whose body had been found in a pickup truck along Butterfield Road. Dental records from the navy had been necessary to identify him.

Music: Steve Winwood's "Roll with It" was at the top of the *Billboard* charts for the week leading up to August 24, 1988.

Movies: The top movie at the box office was *A Nightmare on Elm Street 4: The Dream Warriors.*

TV: *The Cosby Show* was the highest-rated TV series of the week, followed by *A Different World* and *Cheers.*

Books: Tom Clancy's *The Cardinal of the Kremlin* was the *New York Times* bestseller for the week.

Graham, who had grown up in Delaware County and attended school in the town of Gaston, graduated from high school in 1963 and joined the navy. After he was discharged, he returned to Muncie to work at one of the successor plants to Chevrolet on Muncie's southwest side.

A golfer and bowler, the United Auto Workers union member had left work in the afternoon and was last seen around 5:00 p.m. on the day of his death. County coroner Jack Stonebraker said he was killed around 8:00 p.m., although his body wasn't found until his wife made the discovery around 11:30 p.m.

That Graham was shot twice seemed similar not only to the slaying that August of Donald Phillips, who was shot twice and whose remains were found in August in the cab of a pickup truck closer to Muncie, but also the homicide a year later of Bobby Wallace, who was shot twice in a south-side Muncie parking lot.

None of the three cases has been solved.

Following Graham's murder, investigators traveled to Cincinnati and Pennsylvania to check out leads. Closer to home, they went to the automotive plant where Graham worked to check on reports of a dispute over candy that was stolen from Graham's locker.

Cook said in 2014 that police theorized that Graham knew his killer and turned his back to them.

A family member told police that a few weeks before his murder, Graham had installed new deadbolt locks on the doors of the house along Black Cemetery Road. Cook said, "We looked real hard" at members of Graham's family, "but we couldn't prove anything."

One of Graham's stepsons was charged in 1996 with trying to arrange the killing of a county sheriff's deputy to preventing him from testifying at the stepson's upcoming trial on a traffic-related charge. The stepson pleaded guilty in 1997 to conspiracy to commit murder and was given a thirty-year prison sentence.

When the authors of this book posted on Facebook in 2022 that Graham's case would be one that would be included in this book, a woman posted a comment indicating she knew things about the case. One of the authors of this book made arrangements to talk to her for background, but she didn't follow through on her agreement to talk.

If You Have Information

If you have information that could help the investigation into this cold case, contact the Delaware County Sheriff's Office. Sheriff Tony Skinner asks that you go to www.delawarecountysheriff.com and click on the CONTACT tab to find telephone numbers to call as well as a contact form that can be filled out anonymously.

"HE NEEDS TO BE HELD ACCOUNTABLE"

The discovery of Crystal Sedam's body, in a field behind a gas station near the highway exchange of Interstate 69 and Indiana 332, put the investigation into her murder in the hands of Delaware County police investigators.

But county police have long acknowledged that it's likely that the killer had no local connection and neither did Sedam, who was only twenty years old and nineteen weeks pregnant when she and her unborn child were killed and her body found on January 4, 1992.

Sedam worked as a prostitute at truck stops in Indianapolis and Marion County. Investigators believed that she was killed by a man who picked her up there and her body was unceremoniously and cruelly dumped in Delaware County.

This puts Sedam squarely in the category of murder victims who might be victims of a serial killer.

For Sedam's daughter, the accident of the geography of where her mother was killed and where her remains were left has added to the uncertainty and frustration she feels in her quest for justice for her mother.

Shana Forshee was by turns emotional and matter of fact in a 2023 interview for this book, conducted one day before the thirty-first anniversary of the discovery of her mother's body.

Forshee, now thirty-five, was not quite five years old when her mother was killed.

"I feel like my faith has helped me through a lot," she said. "It helped me through a lot, even as a child. A lot of the things I've gone through, it was to help me be there for other people.

Crystal Sedam and her daughter, Shana. *Photo provided by family.*

"I've already forgiven the person who's done this. In order for me to get on with my life, I have to forgive them.

"But I still feel like he needs to be held accountable."

A few times during Delaware County's modern history did an officer of the law discover the remains of a murder victim, but very few times did it happen when the officer was rabbit hunting.

On January 4, 1992, Jason Walker—at the time a county police reserve officer, years later chief deputy of the department—and three relatives, including a brother who was an Indiana State Police officer, were rabbit hunting in a field near the interstate. Walker recalled in a 2015 interview with the authors of this book that he was walking toward where he saw a rabbit run when he saw what he thought was a mannequin.

He quickly determined that what he saw was not a mannequin but the body of a woman who would later be identified as Crystal Sedam.

"I told (my brother) to call the police and he said, 'We are the police.' I told him to call the county and get the coroner."

Walker checked the woman's pulse and found "she was frozen hard."

Walker said he and his hunting party had left their cellphones behind, so he walked up to Indiana 332, trying to stop a motorist who might have one.

Walker, who is Black, grimly speculated why cars swerved to avoid him and continued on their way.

"You got five Black guys with shotguns standing over a dead, naked white girl on the ground," Walker said. "They just kept on rolling."

Crystal Sedam had been working out of Bud's Truck Stop in the Indianapolis area on New Year's Eve. Her husband dropped her off at the truck stop, and she contacted him at about 2:30 a.m. to tell him she would be home soon. When she hadn't arrived in a few hours, he reported her missing by about 1:00 p.m. on New Year's Day.

Her body was found in Delaware County about eighty hours later, on January 4. She wore only a bra and one sock. Delaware County coroner Jack Stonebraker Jr. thought she might have been strangled.

The former gas station in front of the field where Crystal Sedam's body was found. *Photo by Keith Roysdon.*

In the months to come, police arrested first one and then another truck driver in an investigation of drivers that might have killed women. Neither investigation led to charges against whoever killed Sedam.

Over the years, police have considered suspects whom they hoped to connect to Sedam's death. For a 2015 cold case article for the *Star Press* by the authors of this book, investigators cited two men who had been considered suspects.

One was Lonnie Spells, a truck driver from Ohio, who was arrested in the 1992 killing of a prostitute from Memphis, Tennessee. The woman's remains were found along an interstate highway in Texas. Investigators from several states, all working to solve a series of similar killings, focused on the man until trucking company logs showed the man was not near Indiana at the time of Sedam's death.

Another trucker, Sean Patrick Goble, of Asheboro, North Carolina, was arrested in April 1995 and admitted to killing three women he picked up at truck stops in Tennessee and North Carolina. Investigators from ten states thought he might be a viable suspect in cases they were covering.

JANUARY 4, 1992

Local news: A Muncie man was killed and six other people were injured in a multi-car pileup on Interstate 69 near Daleville. A Fayette County judge forbade the Delaware County commissioners from implementing an economic development income tax spending plan drafted by the local chamber of commerce.

Music: The top *Billboard* hit was "Black or White" by Michael Jackson, which dominated the pop charts for most of the month.

Movies: The number-one movie at the box office was *Hook*, the Robin Williams Peter Pan adventure.

TV: The most-watched TV programs were *60 Minutes*, the TV movie *Face of a Stranger*, Monday Night Football and *Cheers*.

Books: *Slow Waltz in Cedar Bend* by Robert Waller, the follow-up to *The Bridges of Madison County*, was the *New York Times* bestseller.

Goble is named in several online compendiums of serial killers, some of which note that he was suspected in many more killings than those of the three women.

In April 1997, Goble was serving two life sentences for murder in what was then the Brushy Mountain State Penitentiary in Petros, Tennessee. The *News-Sentinel* of Knoxville reported that authorities in Alabama would not pursue charges in the killing of two women from Indiana and Ohio and he would remain behind bars for decades.

Before Delaware County investigators could question Goble in connection to Sedam's killing, he stopped cooperating with investigations from other states.

Forshee has herself been caught up in the possibility her mother's killer might have been found.

One night in early 2022, Forshee sent a series of texts to one of the authors of this book, who had spoken to her for the 2015 cold case newspaper article about her mother.

Forshee texted links to news stories about Warren Luther Alexander, a seventy-one-year-old from Mississippi who had been arrested and was to be extradited to North Carolina to be questioned about the 1992 murder of Nona Stamey Cobb. Her body was found along an interstate highway, as Crystal Sedam's body was.

Forshee spoke with police officers about the possibility they might question Alexander about her mother.

Forshee remains optimistic that one day her mother's murder will be solved. It will be a turning point in the life of a woman who's lived with her mother's death every day for all but a few years of her life. But she already feels determined to survive.

"Everything we go through, you can live through it," Forshee said.

IF YOU HAVE INFORMATION

If you have information that could help the investigation into this cold case, contact the Delaware County Sheriff's Office. Sheriff Tony Skinner asks that you go to www.delawarecountysheriff.com and click on the CONTACT tab to find telephone numbers to call as well as a contact form that can be filled out anonymously.

"IF THE TABLES WERE TURNED
AND I WERE MURDERED..."

In the years since Garth Rector was killed in 2008, there have been many theories—and many suspects—connected to his shooting death.

Family and friends and neighbors and police investigators and prosecutors all have thoughts.

The longtime lead investigator in Rector's case has a suspect in mind that he's never talked about publicly before.

In an interview for this book, veteran Delaware County police investigator Kurt Walthour, more recently town marshal for Yorktown, did not cite the person by name but indicated the current circumstances of the suspect.

"We've never put that name out there because it was a rumor," Walthour said. "When something happens, some names come out, and they focus on people who were doing the same things [criminal activity].

"This person is in prison for a long time. At some point, we're going to go speak with him. We'll tell him, 'You'll never get out of prison, so you might as well talk about it.'

"He's in for murder, and for some of these guys who will never get out, a second murder will only increase his street cred in prison. That was the only option, giving him that option, because he'll be 112, if he lives that long, before he gets out."

Walthour has overseen the investigation of Rector's death through thick and thin. Lately, it's been thin.

It's never stopped being heartbreaking for Rector's family, among them his sister, Angie Rector Mock; his wife, Angie; and his daughter, April. They

Garth Rector's survivors, including daughter April and her son, sister Angie Rector Mock and wife Angie. *Photo by Keith Roysdon.*

sat down with the authors of this book in summer 2022, and Angie Rector Mock gave a full interview on the next to last day of the year.

"I want this solved. I want this out there. I'm not giving up on it. If the tables were turned and I were murdered, Garth wouldn't give up on me."

It's likely the circumstances that led to Rector's killing might have been simple: he was well-known and popular, especially with women.

Rector was forty-eight years old in 2008 and renting a house not far from the town of Cowan in southern Delaware County. He and his wife, Angie, had separated, and Rector had been dating.

In the 2016 cold case newspaper article about his slaying, Rector was described by his sister, Angie Rector Mock: "Women liked Garth and Garth liked women."

In a 2022 interview, Mock emphasized that her brother was the type of person whom people liked.

"Garth loved to help people. They went to church at Union Chapel, and he would befriend people and bring them home for dinner. Garth was a very caring person."

Rector was a multisport athlete in school but was known for his wrestling skills. After he graduated and for years after, he would coach teams his daughter, April, played on and coached Mock's son in AAU wrestling. After his years coaching at Central High School, he worked in dining services at Ball State University.

"He was a typical brother, a protector," Mock said. "If I was dating a guy, he would always make sure they were OK. He would call me every morning at 7:00 to tell me to have a good day. He was an amazing father to April.

"He was my big brother," Mock said. "He had his demons. He was not perfect. But he didn't deserve to die, and that doesn't give someone the right to kill him."

When Rector was killed on March 21, 2008, police and family members believe, he was killed by someone who felt very strongly about him, because he was shot five times—twice in the neck and once each in the back and right shoulder and right forearm.

This led some to theorize that Rector was killed in a crime of passion.

In 2016, then–Delaware County prosecutor Jeffrey Arnold said the number of shots certainly indicated Rector's killer knew him and disliked him.

"This is somebody well-connected to Garth Rector," Arnold told the authors of this book. "That leads me to believe there was a lot of emotion and the person will keep quiet."

Just before Rector was killed, he was getting ready to leave for the Indianapolis airport for a family trip to California. He never got to the airport, however. The woman whose family owned the house he was renting—a woman who had dated Rector—saw the lights were off and went over to make sure he hadn't fallen asleep.

She found Rector dead on his kitchen floor.

Dawna Sodders, whose family owned the house and whose sister found Rector, said in a 2022 interview that her sister had been dead for twelve years.

"I love her and she's my sister and I think she went to her grave knowing exactly who did it," she said.

Mock said she has, over the years, had four people in mind who she believes knew many details of the crime, and one of them likely pulled the trigger.

Only one of them is still alive.

Eric Hoffman, the current Delaware County prosecutor, said in a 2022 interview that he thinks solving Garth Rector's murder is still possible.

"It's a tragic case," Hoffman said. "It's one that I think, in time, will be solved. I just think it's going to take some time."

Until that happens, Mock and her family will continue to push for the truth, the longtime investigator on the case said.

MARCH 21, 2008

Local news: It was a big day for local news. Delaware Circuit Court 5 judge Wayne Lennington resigned from the bench, citing health issues but in the wake of an investigation by a state group that oversees judicial conduct. Crowds prepared for Hillary Clinton to speak in the evening at Central High School. And a Muncie man woke up in the back of a garbage truck. He said he had been out drinking with friends the night before and didn't remember how he got in the trash truck.

Music: The *Billboard* top hits were "Love in This Club" by Usher, "With You" by Chris Brown, "Low" by Flo Rida and "Love Song" by Sara Bareilles.

Movies: The top movie at the box office was *Horton Hears a Who*, followed by *Meet the Browns* and *Shutter*.

TV: *Deal or No Deal*, a game show on NBC, was the top program, followed by NCAA basketball and *Lost*, the ABC drama about survivors on an island.

Books: The *New York Times* bestseller chart was topped by *Change of Heart* by Jodi Picoult.

"Angie keeps it out there in the public eye as much as they can," Walthour said. "At some point, there's always the possibility someone might say something."

Walthour hopes the burden of knowing who killed Garth Rector will weigh on someone until they talk.

"When you know you did something like that, it wears you down so much, it takes a toll."

"Garth would be sixty-three in February," Mock said. A resolution to his murder will bring some measure of peace to his loved ones.

"It's not gonna change what happened," she said. "I just want to know why."

If You Have Information

If you have information that could help the investigation into this cold case, contact the Delaware County Sheriff's Office. Sheriff Tony Skinner asks that you go to www.delawarecountysheriff.com and click on the CONTACT tab to find telephone numbers to call as well as a contact form that can be filled out anonymously.

"I WANT THEM TO SIT IN PRISON UNTIL THE DAY THEY DIE"

I t's been said that there's nothing that's worse than a parent burying their child.

It's possible that it's worse when a parent buries their child, and decades later, there's still no resolution to the crime that left their child dead.

William Gene Burton was just sixteen years old when he was shot to death and his body was left at the base of a railroad trestle in Muncie's McCulloch Park on January 24, 1997.

His mother, Vicki Cook, still grieves and still wants justice.

"I would like to see them find out who did it and why they did it," Cook said in a 2022 interview for this book. "I don't want them to get the death penalty. I want them to sit in prison until the day they die.

"I don't want to take their life. I want their lives on hold for the rest of their life."

The morning she was interviewed for this book, Cook said, she spoke to a Muncie police investigator who asked her not to talk about the case for the book.

Cook spoke in general terms, without elaborating on the people she considers suspects in her son's killing, a quarter of a century after his death.

Burton was attending Southside High School the winter he was killed. He was living in a mobile home in southeast Muncie, and he was working part time as a telemarketer selling replacement windows.

Cook lived not far from her son, and the night he was killed, she had come home and noticed a car parked in front of the mobile home where Burton

A cross, carved from a tree stump, near where William Gene Burton's body was found. *Photo by Keith Roysdon*.

lived. She walked toward the car, but the driver abruptly left. She wasn't sure if her son was in the car or not.

Burton was gay, his mother said, and had been seeing a local man not long before his death. That man called Cook the morning after she last saw Burton and said she should go to the park. He believed the body found in the park was wearing Burton's coat.

When Cook got to the park, police kept her at a distance and asked her about what her son was wearing. What she told them made them all but certain his was the body that had been found.

William Burton lay on his left side. Light snow gathered in the folds of his black leather coat. His curly hair was bloody from where he had been shot.

In the weeks that followed the discovery of Burton's body, police worked several leads and theories in their investigation.

One was that Burton had been killed in a gang initiation—someone killing Burton to gain admission to a criminal gang—or that he had been killed by someone he met in the park.

For a 2011 cold case article in the *Star Press* newspaper, veteran police investigator Mike Engle told the authors that Burton would hang out in the park and had friends who did also.

For that 2011 article, Cook expressed frustration at the thought that her son's sexual orientation might have diminished efforts to solve his murder, but Engle said that was not a consideration. "A homicide is a homicide," Engle said. "We throw everything we can at it. Sometimes we run into brick walls and there's nowhere to go."

For a time, investigators hoped that a scrap of paper in Burton's pocket might provide a clue.

According to a report by Delaware County coroner James St. Myer, a search of Burton's pockets yielded only a lip balm, fifty cents in change and a piece of paper with a name and two telephone numbers.

Burton's family members said in 2011 that police hadn't told them about the scrap of paper with the name and numbers.

For the 2011 article, the authors of this book called the two numbers.

The first belonged to a woman who had worked with Burton at a local restaurant. She said Burton probably had her number because he wanted to trade shifts with her.

A railroad trestle near where William Gene Burton's body was found. *Photo by Keith Roysdon.*

JANUARY 24, 1997

Local news: Muncie police launched an internal investigation into the shooting death of a fifty-year-old Muncie woman who had been shot by officers a few days before. In an unrelated case, a Muncie man pleaded not guilty in his initial court appearance after being charged with killing another local man. Delaware County officials said they would investigate a "mess" in a three-year delay in implementing a new 911 dispatching system.

Music: Toni Braxton's "Unbreak My Heart" was the *Billboard* top hit for January and most of February 1997.

Movies: The top movie on January 24, 1997, was *Evita*, the film version of the Broadway hit, with more than $7 million in ticket sales. Other top movie hits included *Metro* and *Jerry Maguire*, which had been in theaters for seven weeks.

TV: Super Bowl XXXI was the top-rated broadcast on TV for the week that included January 24, 1997. Other top shows were *E.R.*, *Seinfeld* and *The X-Files*.

Books: The best-selling book for all of January 1997, according to the *New York Times*, was *Airframe* by Michael Crichton, about an aircraft investigator looking into an in-flight accident.

The other number was disconnected.

In an interview for this book, Cook said a police investigator told her that Muncie police still wanted to solve the case.

She acknowledged she spoke to them about suspects, including people who knew her son. She also cited the gang angle that had been noted early on "but that didn't come up again" until a recent message someone had left.

Her son's murder means that Cook can only speculate what kind of life he might have had as an adult.

"I wonder what he would be doing if he was still here," she said. "He was gay, but he still talked about having a kid. He talked to some girl about wanting a baby. She's dead now, so she's not able to tell anybody what the conversation was about.

"If he was here, I feel like my life would be different," she said, her voice breaking. "Not like it is now."

Cook is very aware of the passage of time since her son was killed.

"I want to find out who killed my kid," she said in 2022. "I'm getting older. I don't want to die not knowing who killed my kid.

"His father's dead, his grandmother's dead, the only two left to see who did it is my brother and me."

IF YOU HAVE INFORMATION

If you have information that could help an investigation into this cold case, contact the Muncie Police Department. Police chief Nate Sloan asks that you contact the Criminal Investigations Division of the Muncie Police Department at 765-747-4867.

A MUNCIE MOTHER
GOES MISSING

While not officially a homicide victim, Ashley Elaine Morris Mullis is perhaps better known to most Muncie and Delaware County residents than most of the slaying victims profiled in this book.

The Muncie woman was twenty-seven when last seen by family members and friends in September 2013.

Since that time, her father, Don Morris, and others have campaigned to keep his daughter's name and image—and her status as a missing person—familiar to community members.

Most involved with the case have long since become convinced that Mullis was a victim of foul play.

Those who knew and loved her maintain there is no chance that the Muncie woman would have willingly abandoned her three children.

Her youngest child, a daughter, was an infant when her mother was last seen.

The baby's father was a local man, long married to another woman and more than thirty years Ashley's senior, who had been involved with Mullis prior to her disappearance.

In a January 2023 interview, Don Morris made it clear he believed the baby's father was the person behind the loss of his daughter.

"He made her disappear so he could steal my granddaughter," Morris said.

Morris said the man had told one of Ashley's family members, and others, that he had given her $10,000—some accounts say $15,000—to start her life over in another part of the country.

SEPTEMBER 2013

Local news: Plans for a $60 million apartment, commercial and parking garage project in the Village, near Ball State University, were unveiled.

Music: Two hits by Miley Cyrus, "We Can't Stop" and "Wrecking Ball," and Katy Perry's "Roar" topped pop music charts in September 2013.

TV: *Sunday Night Football, The Big Bang Theory* and *The Voice* were the 2013–14 TV season's most popular programs.

Movies: The month's most popular motions pictures were *We're the Millers, Cloudy with a Chance of Meatballs 2* and *The Butler*.

Books: *The Cuckoo's Calling*, by Robert Galbraith, and *How the Light Gets In* by Louise Penny were the top-selling fiction books in the United States.

Those who knew her said it was unthinkable Mullis would have willingly ended contact with her children—the baby and her two young sons.

The baby's father—never charged but identified as a person of interest in the case—later relocated to Florida. He reportedly died there, in a Sarasota hospital, in September 2015.

The daughter he shared with Mullis has remained in the custody of her father's family, with Don Morris and his relatives being allowed no visitation.

(The "person of interest" had earlier drawn scrutiny from law enforcement in November 2010 when another young woman from Muncie he befriended died after a fire broke out in a room he had rented for her in a Daleville motel.)

In November 2020, local, state and federal investigators searched property that had been owned by the suspect in western Delaware County, utilizing "cadaver dogs, hand tools and heavy equipment to look for evidence of Ashley," Sheriff Tony Skinner said.

While human remains were not recovered, unspecified items found at the property were submitted to an Indiana State Police laboratory for evaluation.

John Branson, a detective with the sheriff's department, in 2022 acknowledged the death of a "person of interest" had made the Mullis investigation more difficult.

However, he told the *Star Press* newspaper he believed "some people were involved in her disappearance, more than one."

Nearly a decade after Ashley was last seen by her family, the case remains under active investigation.

Until answers are found, Don Morris will continue his efforts to keep the case alive in the minds of the public.

In March 2022, on the occasion of the thirty-sixth anniversary of Ashley's birth, a display was set up outside the Delaware County Justice Center, featuring a poster and T-shirts that focused on the Muncie woman's disappearance, along with a birthday cake.

In 2023, Morris said he and supporters would continue their annual participation in Muncie's St. Patrick's Day parade, keeping the memory of his daughter, and other missing persons, alive.

IF YOU HAVE INFORMATION

If you have information that could help the investigation into this cold case, contact the Delaware County Sheriff's Office. Sheriff Tony Skinner asks that you go to www.delawarecountysheriff.com and click on the CONTACT tab to find telephone numbers to call as well as a contact form that can be filled out anonymously.

THE KILLING OF "BOBBY BLUE"

By all accounts, Robert Nelson was a nice guy. When the eighty-year-old's body was found on the floor of his Kirby Avenue home on December 2, 1996, police initially thought the former custodian had, tragically, killed himself. They thought that in part because he didn't seem to have any enemies who would have motivation to kill him.

Then they discovered that he'd been shot three times—with two different guns.

As longtime Muncie police detective Paul Singleton said in 2016, "I never heard of anyone who shoots himself, says, 'That didn't work' and goes and gets himself another gun and shoots himself again.'"

Nelson grew up in the house on Kirby where his body was found. But between his childhood and his death, he lived history.

He was an army veteran and a member of the Red Ball Express, the trucking outfit mostly composed of African American drivers that delivered supplies to U.S. and Allied military during World War II. Nelson drove a truck on the important route along the Alaska Highway, which was under construction in the final year of the war. At its peak, the Red Ball Express consisted of more than five thousand vehicles that delivered more than twelve thousand tons of supplies a day.

After leaving the army, Nelson returned to Muncie and worked for Muncie Public Library and First Merchants Bank.

He was working at the bank at the time of his death. His sister, Izetta Graham, said she found her brother's body when she went to check on

The house where Robert Nelson was killed. *Photo by Keith Roysdon.*

Robert Nelson. *Photo provided by family.*

DECEMBER 2, 1996

Local news: The *Star Press* noted the death of Herb Khaury, better known as performer Tiny Tim. Khaury had met with a handful of *Star Press* reporters over the years leading up to his death and had joined in making predictions of local elections.

Music: The *Billboard* top hit for the date was "Unbreak My Heart" by Toni Braxton.

Movies: The top movie of the first week of December 1996 was the live-action remake of *101 Dalmatians*, starring Glenn Close.

TV: The top TV broadcast for the date was the Monday Night Football airing of the 49ers and Falcons, followed by *Cosby* and *Melrose Place*.

Books: The *New York Times* bestseller for the period was *The Christmas Box* by Richard Paul Evans.

him. She said that coworkers at the bank called her when he didn't come in to work.

At the time police began investigating Nelson's killing, there were already working on two earlier homicides within three weeks.

When police found Nelson's body, an initial examination of the crime scene might have led to suggestions that he had killed himself. He lay on his back on his living room floor with his hands on his chest and his fingers interlocked. A .38-caliber revolver was on a nearby couch. Police found $170 in cash in his wallet, and they couldn't find any sign of forced entry into his home.

Once Nelson's shirt was removed, police found three bullet wounds. An autopsy found three bullets in his body—one .38 caliber and two .22 caliber.

The investigation that followed grew increasingly indicative of troubles, especially in more than $47,000 in credit card debt from sixteen credit cards. A few days after his death, family members told police that someone had broken into his house and "returned" a credit card. They also reported the discovery of a .22-caliber revolver.

The problem with these new discoveries: police couldn't find evidence to support the idea of a break-in and the couch, where a family member reportedly found the second gun under pillows, had been turned over and thoroughly searched by police.

Singleton, who conducted the investigation, said that while police couldn't narrow the focus to a suspect, Nelson's huge credit card debt was a red flag.

"At eighty, you don't run up that kind of debt on your own," Singleton said.

Glenda Barry, a friend who knew Nelson from his time working as a parking lot attendant at First Merchants Bank, in July 1997 wrote a letter to the editor of the *Star Press* newspaper about her friend.

Barry noted she called him "Bobby Blue" because of the small, bright-blue car he drove. "Bobby Blue was small in stature but tall in all the ways that count. He always had something nice to say and focused on the positive.... The Muncie Police Department is working hard to solve the mystery of a fine man's senseless death. Even if they succeed and bring the responsible party to justice, we can't get back what we have lost with the passing of Robert Nelson."

If You Have Information

If you have information that could help an investigation into this cold case, contact the Muncie Police Department. Police chief Nate Sloan asks that you contact the Criminal Investigations Division of the Muncie Police Department at 765-747-4867.

WHO'S GOT THE FILES? THE ABSENCE OF RECORDS HAMPERS COLD CASE REVIEWS

The two retired cops turned to look at each other at the table at Muncie's Bob Evans restaurant on an early October Saturday.

"He's heard the flood story," they said, simultaneously.

Their words came during a conversation about whether it was possible for investigators to go back and review unsolved murders—cold cases—from thirty, forty or fifty years ago.

The flood story is one that has been repeated over the years, including once in a November 2011 newspaper article written by the authors of this book: a flood in the basement of a local government building sometime before 2000 destroyed old police files.

Over breakfast and coffee, the retired investigators cast some doubt on the story and cited some case files—including some that almost certainly wouldn't have been damaged by the flood in question—that were not in existence anymore.

The lack of police reports and notes and witness statements makes it extremely hard for investigators to review cases.

Some files and evidence are well-preserved: In the early 2010s, when then-Muncie police investigator Nathan Sloan began reviewing files connected to the 1985 killings of two teenagers in Muncie's Westside Park—a case detailed in *The Westside Park Murders*, a 2021 History Press book by the authors of this book—Sloan, later Muncie's police chief, recalled spending two weeks reviewing files from the still-open case.

But other files seemingly no longer exist.

It's hard to say just when old files might have damaged, destroyed or discarded. In case the latter was the cause, it likely would have taken the form of a clerk or deputy being tasked with filling a dumpster with files to make room for more. The same as if files were destroyed.

In the case of damage? The Delaware County Justice Center, the courts-and-jail complex in use from 1992 to about 2018, was notorious for how often court offices, on the first floor, or the 911 dispatch center, in the basement, were subject to leaks from sewer pipes upstairs, sometimes because of inmates in the second-floor jail stopping up toilets with clothing.

In 1991, two instances of sewage floods in the basement were reported. In September 1991, the *Star Press* newspaper reported the second sewage leak of the year that affected the basement of the Justice Center. Delaware County officials estimated that about $25,000 would be needed to replace flooring in the basement and another $5,000 to replace faulty sewage pipe clamps. "Several hundred gallons" of sewage were released in the incident.

At that time, jail inmates were not yet in the building, so the damage couldn't be blamed on them.

The Justice Center basement was, incidentally, where county police records, including case files and evidence files, were stored. The newspaper account did not indicate files were damaged.

In a November 2011 cold case newspaper article, police investigators present and former agreed that file-keeping wasn't good at times, including incidents of files destroyed by disaster.

Then Muncie police sergeant Mike Engle told the authors of this book that it appeared no file existed on William Gump, the subject of a chapter of this book. Engle discounted, to some extent, the idea that the files had been destroyed by water damage.

Richard Heath, who was police chief in the early 1970s, said, "I think they just have poor housekeeping."

Unfortunately, cold case and other police files, kept on paper, are among the first items damaged in the event of disaster. The *New York Times* reported in 2013 that police evidence in warehouses was among the records destroyed by flooding in Hurricane Sandy.

The National Archives keeps a record of lost and damaged files of various kinds reported to the archives and lists not just files damaged by disaster and lost to black mold, for example, but the loss of records due to unauthorized destruction or those that simply went missing when a key record keeper retired.

There's no suggestion of anyone overtly tampering with or destroying files of cold cases in Muncie and Delaware County. There is a strong suggestion from certain quarters that some city or county officials were better at preserving some files than others. Changes from the top, from mayor to police chief to sheriff, mean different priorities for the investigators lower in the ranks.

Police records, including files of investigations, are large and bulky and can present a storage problem. Space is at a premium in most government buildings.

In the late 1990s, under then Delaware County clerk Karen Wenger, the county made arrangements to safely and properly clear 2.3 million pages of court records out of much-needed storage space in the Delaware County Building. In 1997, Wenger reached an agreement with the Muncie Public Library: the library would take those records and digitize them for future inspection by the public.

Among those records was an arrest warrant for John Dillinger, issued in July 1933, a year before the outlaw was killed. The warrant stemmed from the robbery a year earlier of the Bide-A-Wee Inn. Dillinger and cohort Harry Copeland were sought by police for the crime, which saw the tavern's owner, Arley C. Skiff, robbed of $95.

The cost of maintaining records is a consideration: Before Wenger came to an agreement with the library, she received quotes for digitizing the records for the county. One company said it would charge $165,000 for the task.

The transfer of responsibility and upkeep from government to a library isn't possible for many records of criminal investigations: in many cases, the records are confidential and not open to the public. In others, the records need to remain accessible by police investigators, including in cases of long-dormant cold cases that are not yet closed. (Wenger noted that confidential court records would not be transferred to the library.)

Before the files were handed over to the library, nearly five hundred boxes of court records were being stored at county expense in a local warehouse. Having records, particularly police records, stored off site means that they are vulnerable to damage and unauthorized access.

One type of cold case records that are usually consistently well-maintained are coroner's office records.

In 2011, when the authors asked then–Delaware County coroner Scott Hahn about coroner files for cold cases, Hahn pointed to a drawer in a file cabinet in his cramped office. "We have a file of unsolved homicides," Hahn said at the time. "I was shocked when I took office and found this drawer."

The cases in the file cabinet drawer only went back to about 1996, but Hahn was able to find coroner's case files on other, earlier cold cases. The coroner's office has for the most part been careful about preserving the files.

Not every coroner has been meticulous. Hahn told one story about a coroner who simply kept many case files at his home, hardly an ideally secure way of preserving the records.

And in June 1974, the *Muncie Star* reported that the then-Delaware County coroner had failed to file copies of his coroner's case reports—not just on cold cases, but for every type of coroner's case—for more than three years with the county clerk's office, as required by law.

The coroner later properly submitted many of those files. In 2022, Hahn—by this point no longer county coroner—confirmed that the lax record keeping from a half century earlier had indeed occurred.

THE KILLING OF
JAMES TRICKER JR.

Local residents—or, at the very least, those who subscribed to the *Muncie Star*—might have breathed a collective sigh of relief on the final morning of 1960.

"Cab Driver Slaying May Be Solved" read a banner headline on that Saturday's front page.

The brutal killing nine days before—in the early morning hours of December 22, 1960—of thirty-five-year-old James Tricker Jr. had baffled Muncie police and their counterparts with the Delaware County Sheriff's Department.

The frozen remains of the Muncie man, an employee of Yellow Checker Cab Co., had been found by a motorist along Delaware County Road 400-E, about a quarter-mile south of McGalliard Road.

After seeing the body—Tricker's head was on the east edge of the road, which was nearly impassable due to drifting snow; the victim's feet were facing east—Ralph Vest went to a nearby farmhouse for help. The Delaware County jail received a call reporting Vest's grim discovery at 5:55 a.m.

The *Star* on December 23 would publish a photo, provided by the sheriff's department, that showed emergency personnel at the scene, placing Tricker's remains on a stretcher.

Tricker had been shot once, in the left wrist, but his death had been the result of a skull fracture, caused by blunt force trauma, Delaware County coroner Warren Bergwall said after an autopsy.

(Investigators would later determine Tricker's wristwatch was missing. And his wallet, believed to have contained more than seventy dollars the night of his death, held no money.)

The Yellow Checker Cab dispatcher's last contact with Tricker had been about midnight, when he was sent to pick up a fare at the 300 Club, at Twenty-Fourth and Madison Streets.

The dispatcher reported Tricker missing to Muncie police at 3:30 a.m. About five minutes after that, an officer found his cab—with its radio on and the keys in the ignition—at Gilbert and Jefferson Streets.

Also that morning, authorities in Valparaiso, 160 miles northwest of Muncie, had apprehended four young men—three from Gary and one from Chicago—after a chase that saw the suspects crash a pink Cadillac.

The vehicle belonged to Muncie grocer Iva Mae Bradley and had been stolen the night before from the 1700 block of East Centennial Avenue.

It was decidedly not a good day to be caught in a car stolen from Muncie.

A sheriff's deputy, Dale Horr, and a city police detective, Melvin Miller, were sent to Valparaiso to return the quartet to Muncie to be questioned in the Tricker case.

(Miller had previously arrested one of the Gary men, Dock Wheeler Jr.—who had relatives living in Muncie—for stealing items from a railroad boxcar.)

On December 24, James Tricker was laid to rest in Elm Ridge Cemetery.

An army veteran of both World War II and the Korean War, Tricker left behind his pregnant wife, Charline; two children from a previous marriage, Richard and Rebecca; and his mother, Helen Johnson.

Within a few days, authorities had determined the car thieves from northwestern Indiana played no role in Tricker's killing. In January, they would plead guilty to local counts of auto theft.

(One of those suspects, and also one of the slaying victim's coworkers at the cab company, had been taken to Indiana State Police headquarters in Indianapolis for lie-detector tests.)

Detectives also tried, but failed, to link the homicide to a November 26 mugging of Muncie barber Oval T. "Tom" Pennington, in an alley near Frank Foundry. The thirty-three-year-old Pennington was robbed of $100 and lost an eye as a result of a beating.

"So far, we have not come out with the first bit of tangible evidence as to the identity of [Tricker's] killer," an investigator told the *Star* on December 29.

Chief Deputy Sheriff Joe Dooley, meanwhile, said investigators had knocked on so many doors—within two miles of where Tricker's body was found, and within two blocks of where his cab was discovered—that their "knuckles are bleeding."

The following day, however, a phone call from Texas would appear to break the case wide open.

On December 18—four days before the Tricker killing—three prisoners at the Madison County jail in Anderson escaped, reportedly by leaping from a second-story window.

A week later, on Christmas Day, the escapees—Donald N. Carlson, twenty-seven; James Roy Grover, thirty-one; and Haston Lee Winnett, twenty—broke into a diner in the small town of Tulia, Texas, about 50 miles south of Amarillo, and 1,080 miles from the Madison County jail.

When Tulia's assistant police chief, forty-one-year-old Robert Potter, tried to apprehend the burglars, the men were eating turkey they had found in the restaurant and trying to break into a jukebox.

Winnett—who, with Grover, had been jailed for breaking into a Madison County school—shot the officer dead.

When the trio were captured later that holiday, in a roadblock in an isolated section of the Texas Panhandle, they had sixteen guns, including that of the slain police officer.

They reportedly confessed to Potter's slaying.

Within a few days, Carlson—a native of Johnstown, Pennsylvania, who was in the Anderson jail after being linked to an insurance scam—had another confession to make.

Carlson told Texas authorities he and the other men had been in Muncie the night of December 21–22—and that he had robbed and killed James Tricker.

A contingent of Muncie, Delaware County and Indiana State Police investigators flew to Texas, in an ISP plane, to question Carlson.

The Pennsylvania man provided them with a signed statement, indicating he had approached Tricker at the near-downtown intersection where his cab was found, and forced him at gunpoint behind the wheel of a stolen car.

His two fellow escapees were drunk and sleeping in that vehicle's back seat, Carlson said.

After forcing Tricker to drive to an isolated area east of Muncie, Carlson reported, he ordered the cab driver out of the vehicle, intending to rob him.

Carlson said Tricker was shot, accidentally, when the Muncie man tried to gain possession of his captor's shotgun. Carlson said he then went back to the stolen car, retrieved a piece of pipe, and twice struck Tricker in the head.

"I didn't mean to kill the man," Carlson added. He also reported he had thrown the shotgun and pipe into a ravine in Tennessee while en route to Texas.

Delaware County prosecutor Gene Williams at first said he was "a little suspicious" about Carlson's confession.

"I can see where a fellow charged with killing a policeman in Texas might be glad to come back to Indiana and face trial for killing a cab driver," the prosecutor said.

(Others speculated Carlson hoped a trip back to Indiana might provide more and better opportunities for again escaping.)

While local investigators said it was unlikely Carlson—facing a life sentence, if not execution, in the officer's slaying—would ever stand trial in Indiana, they were increasingly convinced they had found Tricker's killer.

City police detective Ernest Sutton told the *Evening Press* he was "absolutely" certain Carlson was telling the truth.

"He told us too many things he otherwise couldn't have known," Sutton said, including the fact that the slaying victim's shirttail had been hanging out.

Some local witnesses believed they had seen Carlson and his cohorts at the Pasttime Bar, on South Walnut Street, the night of Tricker's death.

"Tricker case is closed," an *Evening Press* headline read on January 7.

Sheriff Jack Young told the newspaper his department would end its investigation.

(However, Deputy Paul Gardner "privately" remained convinced Carlson was not the killer, the story indicated.)

"Carlson's statement ended 11 days of intensive investigation by city, county and state officials," the *Star* reported.

On January 15, to no one's surprise, Coroner Bergwall officially declared Tricker's death to be the result of a homicide.

"It is the opinion of the coroner that the deceased was struck on the head by some blunt object, was shot in the left wrist and left to die on the highway," Bergwall was quoted in articles that identified Donald Carlson as the likely killer.

Jay Dull's first public exposure as a lawbreaker came early.

On December 1, 1949, the day before his thirteenth birthday, Dull escaped from the Delaware County jail—for the second consecutive day.

The Muncie youth had been quickly recaptured after his first escape. Dull's second bid for freedom, however, was more successful. He turned up a week later at his father's home in Miami, Florida.

Top: Walter Line. *Bottom*: Jay Dull. *From the authors' collection.*

Newspapers articles reflect only that the twelve-year-old Dull was being held "for questioning" in the jail—presumably in an area reserved for juveniles—at the time of those escapes.

(Dull was actually in the news even before that. In June 1947, a major search was conducted for the then ten-year-old, whose family feared he had drowned while swimming in Buck Creek. He turned up unharmed, less than two miles from his family's West Sixteenth Street home, two days later.)

As he progressed through his teens and into early adulthood, Dull was often in trouble, most frequently for stealing cars. As a result, he would spend stretches of time at the Indiana Boys School, the Indiana State Farm and, finally, the Pendleton Reformatory.

Dull's brief stint in the army ended with a court martial for going AWOL. At some point in the late 1950s, Dull served time in a Colorado prison for a robbery conviction.

An accomplice in many of Dull's local criminal activities, and his codefendant in several resulting cases, was Walter Gerald Line, also born in Muncie in 1936.

One of their joint prosecutions, when they were both eighteen, stemmed from the 1954 theft of a Muncie minister's car from a downtown parking lot.

Line's convictions had also resulted in multiple periods of incarceration, at the Boys School and later the Reformatory.

Line's most recent prison stint had ended in September 1960. Dull—doing time for a 1959 conviction for possession of a handgun, stolen from a safe at the North Star Drive-In, 2324 South Madison Street—was granted his freedom the following month.

On the night of January 10, 1961, a car belonging to Veva Peters Rainey, mother of a city police officer, was stolen from in front of her home in the 700 block of West Powers Street.

The vehicle was later returned; its odometer reflected a fifty-mile overnight trip. Because a spare key was missing from the car's sun visor, it was anticipated the vehicle would be "borrowed" again.

The following evening—January 11, twenty days after James Tricker's death—Muncie police detectives Jack Stonebraker Jr. and John Nicewander were "staking out" the vehicle outside the Rainey home. About 11:30 p.m., two men—soon to be identified as Jay Dull and Walter Line—entered the car.

Stonebraker, on foot, approached the vehicle and ordered the men to stop. Dull, behind the wheel of the stolen auto, swerved and tried to run the investigator down.

After Dull crashed into the officers' nearby car and then continued with his bid to flee, the detectives opened fire.

Dull was shot in the neck. Line was wounded in the back. The stolen car rolled to a stop at Powers and Council Streets.

Both men were taken by ambulance to Ball Memorial Hospital, where Dull would remain, under police guard, for several days, for a time listed in critical condition.

He and Line were quickly linked to, and charged with, a pair of recent armed robberies, at a liquor store at Eighth Street and Hoyt Avenue, and a grocery in the 2300 block of Port Avenue.

Authorities found two weapons in the vehicle—a "razor-sharp paring knife" in Dull's coat pocket, and, on the car's front seat, a sawed-off double-barrel shotgun. (Investigators suggested there was evidence an attempt was made to shoot that firearm at Nicewander and Stonebraker, but the weapon misfired.)

As some point over the next week, David "Dago" Thomas, a city police captain, was playing a hunch when he decided to aim a new line of questioning at Line, whose bullet wound was far less severe than that suffered by Dull.

Thomas would later say a "nervous reaction" by Line, when questioned about the sawed-off shotgun, "convinced him he was on the right track."

Line would fairly quickly acknowledge he and Dull had been responsible for the Tricker slaying.

The Muncie man said he had bought the shotgun from a teen, in the Hyde Park addition in Liberty Township, and later sawed off portions of the weapon's stock and barrel at a relative's home.

The night of the slaying, Line told Thomas, he and Dull spent time in a downtown cigar store, then picked up the shotgun from a nearby hiding place and decided to "roll" someone.

Their target eventually became Tricker, who had picked the ex-convicts up in his cab and at first was told to deliver them to the Oasis Bar & Grill at Burlington and Memorial Drives.

Before they reached the tavern, however, Tricker was shown the shotgun and told to move out of the driver's seat. Dull eventually drove the cab to the scene of the slaying, Line said.

It was Dull, he added, who had inflicted the victim's injuries.

On January 18, a still-hospitalized Dull signed a confession of his own.

He maintained he had intended to strike Tricker in the head with the shotgun when it accidentally discharged, wounding the victim in the wrist. Dull said he then struck the wounded man twice in the head with the gun's stock.

"All I wanted to do was knock him out," Dull said. "I had intended to stun the driver so he would not know which direction we (went)….I wanted to make sure Line and I got back to Muncie before he did."

But with the temperature the night of the slaying hovering around zero, leaving behind a slightly injured person, as Dull claimed he had intended, could have proved lethal. Tricker, with both a gunshot wound and a severely fractured skull, never had a chance.

Dull also told police Tricker, before being attacked, had pleaded with him not to abandon him along the county road under such conditions.

"Don't make me walk," the victim purportedly said. "I won't tell anyone [about the robbery]."

Dull also provided detectives with the evidence they needed to prove his guilt.

Based on that information, authorities were able to track down the two watches stolen from Tricker the night of his death. (Dull had sold one of the timepieces to a man in a bar for two dollars.)

Detectives also went to the Huron Hotel, at Main and Jefferson Streets, where the suspects had rented a room, presumably with Tricker's cash—and signing in as "Jay Dull and friend"—hours after the killing.

As Dull had promised, in the hotel they found the cap of the shotgun shell fired at Tricker behind a bathroom mirror.

As for Donald Carlson, local investigators said they no longer believed his claims that he had killed Tricker—although they did not rule out he and the other Madison County jail escapees had been in Muncie that night.

"This time, detectives have physical evidence to prove the confessions are not a hoax," the *Evening Press* reported.

Line told detectives "Jay and I thought about going to Mexico" after the Tricker homicide but decided to delay that trip until Line could attend a meeting with his parole officer on January 13.

Had the pair more promptly headed for the Mexican border, it's possible Carlson, not Dull, would be remembered as the man who killed James Tricker.

A day after he signed his confession, Dull was transferred from the hospital to the Delaware County jail.

(And for historical perspective, a day after Dull's transfer to the jail, John F. Kennedy—who had campaigned in Muncie the previous April and October—was sworn in as the nation's thirty-fifth president.)

On February 18, Dull was present for the empaneling of the Delaware County grand jury that would indict him and Line on first-degree murder charges. Line had waived his right to attend the proceedings.

(The panel would also issue two other indictments stemming from local homicides. One of those indicted was a fifteen-year-old boy who, after attending a Harlem Globetrotters' game at the Muncie Fieldhouse on December 16, "for no apparent reason" had punched another youth in the head outside nearby Orv's Drive-In. The other youth, also fifteen, collapsed the following day, the victim of brain injuries that would soon cause his death. His assailant's case would be referred to juvenile court authorities. Also indicted was a forty-three-year-old Muncie woman who on February 17 had fatally shot an unruly customer in the East Centennial Avenue chicken restaurant she co-owned with her husband. She was later convicted of manslaughter.)

On March 22, a Delaware Circuit Court jury of eight men and four women was seated to hear the state's case against Dull and Line.

During the selection proceedings, the prospective jurors had been questioned at length about their willingness to impose a death sentence if warranted.

(Judge Alva Cox had also "severely admonished" a Warner Gear employee trying to get out of jury duty. Cox said he was tired of executives at the factory trying to keep their "key personnel" off juries. "We need them, too," the judge said. "The county needs their services, and so do the defendants and the state.")

Trial coverage indicated jurors "didn't flinch" when shown "colored, bloody" photos of Tricker's remains, showing the bullet wound in his left wrist and his fatal head injuries.

City police captain Thomas was called to the stand to read aloud the statements about the killing the defendants had given to police.

Line's attorney, Victor M. Bruell, tried to persuade jurors his client had been insane at the time of the homicide.

Two court-appointed physicians, however, maintained Line—who stopped attending school after the seventh grade—knew the difference between right and wrong, although one acknowledged he was "easily influenced."

Dr. Henry Elga Bibler told jurors Line "bordered between [being] a high-grade moron and low normal intelligence."

A local school administrator testified records showed Line had failed most of his courses while in elementary school but had been routinely promoted to the next grade with his classmates.

Both defendants "sported fresh haircuts" the day they took the witness stand.

Line, for his part, acknowledged handing Dull the shotgun used to fatally injure Tricker.

For Dull's defense team—attorneys Clarence Benadum and Frederick McClellan—the objective was not an acquittal by reason of insanity or otherwise. Instead, they sought to keep their client out of the Indiana State Prison's electric chair.

"I'm sorry for it," Dull told the jury about Tricker's slaying. "But now it's too late to be sorry."

Deputy Prosecutor Dick Clapp took note when Dull testified he and Line had the sawed-off shotgun for "protection."

"You didn't need protection against Mr. Tricker, did you?" Clapp demanded of the witness.

Dull conceded he had needed no such protection.

"Did Mr. Tricker ask you for mercy?" the deputy prosecutor asked.

"I believe he did," Dull said.

"Tell the jury what kind of mercy you gave him," Clapp told the defendant.

"Very little," Dull responded.

In the courtroom gallery, the victim's widow—in a "maternity garment," an article said—sobbed as Dull described her husband's last moments, saying he had struck Tricker in the head "twice, I think."

Charline Tricker had earlier shed tears on the witness stand when asked to identify her late husband's watches.

During the trial, deputies inspected the contents of the purses of Dull's mother, Mildred Haskett—and Dull's wife, Helen, who said they had been estranged at the time of his most recent arrest—before allowing them to join him at the defense table.

Haskett took the stand to recount her son's troubled life.

"I tried to bring him up right, and did all I could for him, but something went wrong somewhere," she told the jury.

Closing arguments in the case were held on Friday, March 24.

"You can fry them, if you choose," one of Dull's lawyers, the always colorful Benadum, told the jury. "But if you have seen them die in the electric chair, as I have in Ohio, and have seen them squirm and the smoke curl up from their bodies, I think you will not want such a scene on your minds."

Benadum placed his hands on the shoulders of Line and Dull and said their actions had been "wrong, dastardly wrong."

"[But] I can't believe they are all bad," he said. "Give them a chance. If they behave themselves, they will have a chance to leave prison in fifteen or twenty years."

Deputy Prosecutor Clapp had a different assessment of the defendants, saying they had failed to display "one element of human decency at any time."

"Something must be done to convince the criminal element Delaware County is not the easy spot of the earth, the place where murders may be committed without fear of the death penalty being inflicted," Clapp said.

Line's attorney, Bruell, urged the panel to find his client was insane at the time of the killing.

"If their executions could bring Tricker back, I think it would be the proper thing to do," he said. "However, it will not bring him back. It would [only] mean the killing of two more."

"Dull showed no mercy for Tricker," Deputy Prosecutor James Jordan said in his summation. "Dull and Line were the judge, jury and executioner so far as Tricker was concerned.

"Here, we have a judge. You are a jury, and the executioner should be summoned."

The jury began its deliberations that afternoon at 2:40 p.m.

About eight hours later, a little after 10:30 p.m., Dull and Line were returned to the courtroom to hear the jury's verdicts. They were handcuffed together, the *Star* reported, and "tied, with a heavy log chain held by a deputy."

Perhaps due to the late hour, after a weeklong trial that kept the courtroom gallery filled, only about twenty-five spectators were on hand to hear both men found guilty of first-degree murder.

The jury recommended that Line be "confined for the rest of his natural life."

Dull, they said, should be put to death.

The *Evening Press* reported Dull "closed his eyes and clenched his teeth" when the sentencing recommendations to Judge Cox were announced.

His wife and mother sobbed.

Line's mother, Mrs. Robert Mohler, fainted and was taken by ambulance to Ball Hospital.

Jurors later said they had spent most of the hours deliberating in an eleven-to-one deadlock. A single juror had been reluctant to recommend a death sentence for Dull.

Eventually, she relented and voted with the majority.

"I made up my own mind," the tearful woman told the *Press*. "I pray we have done the right thing."

The recommendations made the court-ordered punishment for Dull and Line all but a formality, but Cox would not sentence the men for a month.

Officials at the jail feared the convicts, particularly Dull, now might try to take their own lives.

The men were stripped of all clothing, as a "precautionary measure against any plans for suicide," authorities said.

After two days, Sheriff Young permitted Dull and Line to don underwear and to "mingle" with other inmates in the jail's "bullpen" twice each day.

At a brief hearing on the morning of April 24, Judge Cox sentenced Walter Line to life in prison.

The judge then rejected Dull's appeal for a new trial and ordered that the Muncie man be executed "before the hour of sunrise on October 9, 1961."

Reporters would later note the first death sentence in Delaware County history had "quashed a legend" that Muncie founder Goldsmith Gilbert "forbade" capital punishment in a deed donating the courthouse square to the county.

Dull was reported to be amiable a short time later as he chatted with his wife and mother through a small window in the door of his cell.

(A little more than a month later, Helen Dull would sue the condemned killer for divorce, at his request, she told the media.)

At 10:05 a.m., Dull and Line were led to a waiting sheriff's car for the three-hour trip to Michigan City.

Dull had a parting gift for his mother—his lighter and cigarettes.

"Well, I don't guess I'll need these now," he told her.

Jay Dull would never be executed.

The first stay of his death sentence was issued in September 1961, the same month Charline Tricker gave birth to her late husband's third child, Carolann.

In May 1963, for the third time in less than two years, a court order was signed authorizing Dull to be put to death by electrocution. But in each instance, appeals resulted in the execution being postponed.

On May 19, 1972, Dull was back in the Delaware County jail, in town for a series of appeals hearings. Oddly, given his status as a convicted—and at least, technically, still a condemned—killer, Dull was chosen by then-sheriff James P. Carey to serve as a jail trusty.

That day, Dull seized a deputy's .38-caliber pistol, took two deputies and a young reporter—Larry Lough, a generation later the first editor of the *Star Press*—as hostages and, with two fellow prisoners, escaped from the jail.

He and his accomplices were quickly recaptured.

In May 1973, a Delaware Circuit Court jury found Dull guilty of kidnapping, and he received a life sentence.

However, the U.S. Supreme Court later overturned the conviction and sentence, ruling Dull had not been brought to trial in a timely fashion.

The Supreme Court had already delivered good news for Dull—and, among others, fellow Indiana Boys School alumnus Charles Manson—a few weeks after his 1972 escape when it revoked all pending death sentences nationwide. In 1975, Dull was officially resentenced for the Tricker slaying, this time to life in prison.

Eight years later, in 1983, after more than twenty-two years of incarceration, Dull was granted parole and released from prison.

As a "lifer," Walter Line's years in prison were less dramatic than those of his codefendant.

He did escape from a work detail outside the state prison in July 1968. He was captured a month later in Muncie, where he was working for a tree-trimming business under an assumed name.

Line was granted parole in 1982 and released. He married and spent much of the next three decades in Texas, working in construction. Widowed, Line returned to Delaware County to stay with a relative not long before he died at age seventy-six in July 2013.

Line's death came ten days after that of John Nicewander, one of the two Muncie police detectives who more than a half-century earlier had captured Dull and Line.

(The other detective, Jack Stonebraker Jr., had gone on to enjoy a long political career, winning election as coroner, auditor and county commissioner.)

Donald Carlson, the Pennsylvania-born con artist and jail-breaker who for a time convinced local authorities he had killed James Tricker, received a life sentence for his role in the Christmas 1960 slaying of the Texas lawman.

DECEMBER 22, 1960

Local news: Five members of a Hartford City family, including four children and their mother, were killed when a fire broke out in their home three days before Christmas. Two other children who suffered severe burns in the fire later died in an Indianapolis hospital.

Music: Topping the *Billboard* Hot 100 throughout December 1960 was "Are You Lonesome Tonight" by Elvis Presley.

TV: *Gunsmoke*, *Wagon Train* and *Have Gun—Will Travel* were the 1960–61 TV season's most popular programs.

Movies: *Swiss Family Robinson*, released on December 22, by a wide margin would be the month's most popular motion picture.

Books: *Hawaii* by James Michener was the top-selling fiction book in the United States.

Carlson died in the Huntsville Prison in September 1986 and is buried on the grounds of the Texas prison, under a cross that carries no name.

As for Jay Dull, while he wasn't destined to be executed, it would be his fate to die behind bars. In 1988, after five years of freedom, he stopped reporting to his parole officer. In 1991, he was recaptured and returned to prison.

His efforts to win another chance at freedom would give James Tricker's children—who weren't consulted before Dull's release in 1983—opportunities to represent their father and confront his killer at a series of parole hearings.

Dull's requests for parole—the last considered at a hearing in 2007, when Dull was seventy—were denied.

In June 2009, a terminally ill Dull was moved from what had been known as the Pendleton Reformatory—when he was first incarcerated in the mid-1950s after he and Line stole cars in Muncie—to the New Castle Correctional Facility. He died, at age seventy-two, in that institution's infirmary, a few hours after the transfer.

Contacted by a reporter, Richard Tricker—who was thirteen when Dull killed his father—expressed relief that after nearly a half-century, the saga had come to an end.

"I'd just like to say I'm glad it's over," said Tricker, who would die in 2012. "And I'm glad that he got the sentence that was given to him.…He didn't die in the electric chair, but at least he died in prison."

"WHAT GOES AROUND..."

Cecil John Carter, to his credit, was an army veteran of World War II. He was also, according to local authorities, something of a career criminal.

On April 20, 1989, Carter at age seventy became a homicide victim, in a case that more than three decades later remains unsolved.

And he was also quite possibly a killer. Despite a brief period in which he implicated himself in an acquaintance's slaying, he was never convicted of that crime.

Born in Muncie in 1918, Carter's criminal activities—including an apparent propensity to burglarize gas stations—resulted in a stay in an Indiana prison before his military service, which began with his enlistment in the army about six weeks before the December 1941 attack on Pearl Harbor.

He remained in the army through the war, finally returning to civilian life in December 1945.

By August 1947, Carter was back in prison after again breaking into Muncie gas stations. On the day he was transported to the Indiana Reformatory in Pendleton, he married Muncie resident Lora Mae Willis, a welder.

The couple divorced in April 1956. Lora Mae told a judge her husband "drank to excess and quarreled and argued constantly," according to a report in the *Muncie Evening Press*.

That divorce coverage aside, Cecil Carter's life produced few headlines in the 1950s, when he worked for a time at Warner Gear, and the 1960s, which saw him employed at Ball Memorial Hospital.

Street sign near the Cecil Carter murder scene. *Photo by Keith Roysdon.*

On March 19, 1971, Carter called the Muncie Police Department and said he wanted to talk to an officer "about something that has been bothering me for a long time."

At the police station, he told a story he had earlier shared with his wife of four years, Marie. Carter said fourteen years earlier, he had killed Marie's first husband, Horace J. Whitworth.

Carter said he and the forty-seven-year-old Whitworth had been "running around" together on an evening in November 1957 before they clashed when Whitworth had twice refused to lend Carter money to purchase a drink.

According to Carter, he struck Whitworth in the head with an iron pipe, then drove his victim home, to the 1600 block of South Jefferson Street, where he left the mortally wounded man in his front yard—after removing cash from Whitworth's wallet.

Whitworth was unconscious when he was later found outside his home. About nine hours after that, he died, from complications of a head injury, at Ball Memorial Hospital.

The dead man's wallet, containing no cash, also was found in his front yard.

The wallet's discovery aside, Muncie police in 1957 said they believed Whitworth had been the victim of an accident, falling and striking his head on a water-meter cover after arriving home from a tavern.

Carter's confession in March 1971 drew far more attention from local newspapers than Whitworth's death had.

"Man confessed to Muncie slaying 14 years ago," read a front-page headline in the *Evening Press*.

Carter was jailed and preliminarily charged with first-degree murder.

By the time he appeared at an initial court hearing the next week, however, Carter had changed his story.

"I was teasing my wife about the killing and I was lying to police," he testified.

Police said that absent the confession, they had no evidence linking Carter to Whitworth's death.

A Delaware County grand jury a few weeks later heard evidence in the case. No indictment was returned.

City police in 1971 appeared confused about the chronology of Carter's dealings with wife Marie and her first husband.

They noted Carter and Marie had not married until 1967, making it unlikely he even knew Whitworth, who had died a decade earlier.

However, the 1967 marriage was the second time the couple had wed. Carter and Marie had also married in August 1956, fifteen months before Horace Whitworth died.

One Muncie officer in 1971 also told the *Evening Press* that Marie had only been married to Whitworth for a short time, many years before his death.

However, court records reflect they were married for considerably longer than a decade and had four children together before divorcing in the late 1940s.

Their daughter, Vaneda Jean Whitworth Manderbach, was eighty when she was interviewed by the *Star Press* for a cold case article in 2014 on the deaths of her father and Cecil Carter.

Forty-three years after his recanted confession, she continued to believe her stepfather "was involved in the death of my father."

"I thought he was capable of it because he did not like my dad," Manderbach said. "I just had bitter feelings toward him."

In December 1971—only nine months after her husband's confession had briefly put their personal life under scrutiny—Marie Carter was killed in a one-vehicle accident on Interstate 69 near Anderson.

Cecil Carter's grave. *Photo by Douglas Walker.*

During his seventeen years as a widower, Cecil Carter would return to a life of crime.

About 2:00 a.m. on April 20, 1989, police were sent to a report of a disturbance at 911 West Charles Street.

When they arrived, officers found an apartment, on the first floor of the five-unit building, engulfed in flames.

When the blaze was extinguished, Carter's body was found on his kitchen floor.

Glenn Scroggins, arson investigator for the Muncie Fire Department, reported he found evidence at least three fires had been set in Carter's two-room apartment, one of them on the victim's bed.

A week later, Delaware County coroner Jack Stonebraker Jr. ruled Carter's death was a homicide.

While he had a fatal level of carbon monoxide in his blood system, an autopsy showed Carter had also suffered multiple skull fractures in what investigators believed had been a beating.

Muncie police detectives believed robbery was the motive for the homicide. They described Carter as a small-time drug dealer, loan shark and bootlegger, selling marijuana—for three dollars a joint, or two for five dollars—and his own prescription medications.

"He was known to flash his money and flash his drugs," Norm Irelan, a Muncie police lieutenant, said in the wake of the slaying. "He wasn't real discreet about his transactions."

Irelan would later say the investigation was hampered by a lack of cooperation from would-be witnesses.

"Everyone likes to lie," he said. "They want to know what we know first, and if we know it, they'll admit to it. Sometimes when you get people who are associated with people involved in criminal activity, you have trouble getting information."

Possible suspects developed in the case included Warren Edward Ellington, a twenty-seven-year-old ex-con who lived across the street from Carter.

Ellington was arrested on unrelated warrants soon after the slaying. Health problems then saw him transferred from the Delaware County jail to Ball Memorial Hospital.

On May 10, while police were awaiting the results of tests on blood and hair evidence recovered from the scene of Carter's death, Ellington walked away from the hospital.

That set the stage for a high-profile manhunt that lasted for five days, until Ellington surrendered—initially not to police but to Joe Canan, a veteran reporter for the *Evening Press*.

Before he was returned to the jail, Ellington told the reporter he had met Carter three times, purchasing marijuana from him once.

News coverage speculating on his possible involvement in the homicide made it "pretty hard to show my face around town," he said.

APRIL 20, 1989

Local news: Developers sought a zoning change to allow construction of a shopping center along East McGalliard Road, prompting speculation Walmart or Cub Foods might have plans to open stores in Muncie.

Music: Madonna's "Like a Prayer" topped pop charts the last two weeks of April in 1989.

TV: *Roseanne* was American's most popular TV program, as reflected in Nielsen ratings for the week of April 17–22 in 1989. Other highly rated shows that week included *The Cosby Show*, *Golden Girls* and *The Wonder Years*.

Movies: *Field of Dreams*, which opened on April 21, was the month's top performing film in the United States. Next on the list were *Pet Sematary* and *Major League*.

Books: *The Satanic Verses* by Salman Rushdie topped bestseller lists in April 1989.

When the results of the laboratory tests made their way to Muncie, they provided police with no evidence linking Ellington—or any other suspects—to the crime.

In 2014, Steve Stanley, by then retired after nearly three decades with the Muncie Police Department, told the *Star Press* he continued to believe there was legitimate evidence in Carter's death that pointed to Ellington.

"We had one main suspect from the start and we followed that up and took it to the prosecutor, and they refused to prosecute," Stanley said, adding that he later tried to persuade subsequent prosecutors to pursue the case.

Ellington's problems with the law continued after Carter's slaying. In 1997, he was convicted of robbing a south-side restaurant. Five years later, he was sentenced to twelve years in prison after he was found to be in possession of a sawed-off shotgun.

He was out of prison by 2014, when he responded to the *Star Press* article on Carter's slaying by leaving a profane message on a reporter's voicemail.

Warren Ellington died at a local healthcare facility in January 2021. Most of the law enforcement professionals who investigated Carter's killing are also gone, including Stanley, who died in May 2022.

Following the 1989 homicide, Cecil Carter was laid to rest in Tomlinson Cemetery south of Muncie. His grave—next to that of wife Marie—is marked with a tombstone that notes his military service.

Understandably, Carter's passing was not mourned by stepdaughter Vaneda Manderbach, who believed his confession to having killed her father in 1957.

"It's a terrible thing to say and God forgive me for saying it, but the life [Carter] lived, I felt it was justice," she told the *Star Press* in 2014.

IF YOU HAVE INFORMATION

If you have information that could help an investigation into this cold case, contact the Muncie Police Department. Police chief Nate Sloan asks that you contact the Criminal Investigations Division of the Muncie Police Department at 765-747-4867.

"THE PROVERBIAL MONSTER LURKING IN THE DARKNESS"

Its savagery and circumstances rank it among the most horrific slayings in Muncie history.

It was, for a time, an unsolved cold case. But the man responsible would ultimately be held accountable.

On Christmas Eve 2009, thirty-five-year-old Monica Lee "Nikki" Brown was killed inside her South Kinney Avenue home.

With no arrests being made in the immediate wake of the slaying, Muncie police detectives released few details about the killing.

Only years later was it revealed the victim had been stabbed about seventy times and that her throat had been slashed.

Investigators believed the homicide took place in the predawn hours. Her killer left Brown's two youngest children—a two-year-old boy and a six-month-old girl—in the home with their mother's remains.

When Brown's two older daughters—ages seventeen and eleven—arrived at the home for a visit about 11:15 a.m. that day, they found their younger brother in their mother's bedroom, "trying to wake up Mommy," city police captain Mark Vollmar later recalled.

Brown was a Southside High School graduate who had worked as a certified nursing assistant. But family members would later acknowledge drugs—and potentially dangerous associates—had been present in the final months of the Muncie woman's life.

Monica Brown and her family. *Photo provided by family.*

"She wouldn't turn anyone away," Brown's mother, Kim Hill, told the *Star Press* in an article published on the second anniversary of her daughter's death. "She felt everybody deserved a second chance."

(Sadly, Hill died in 2014, before seeing her daughter's killer charged and convicted.)

Brown had recently twice gone to Florida on a mission to build up a large supply of OxyContin, a powerful painkiller frequently prescribed to cancer patients, by obtaining prescriptions from numerous physicians in the Sunshine State.

Muncie police would learn she was selling the drug out of her home, a block east of Hoyt Avenue on the city's near-south side.

"I tried everything I could," Kim Hill told the *Star Press* in 2011. "I told her not to let those people come over there, not to let them live there. I was trying to do something to keep her out of the mess she was in, but she was getting deeper and deeper into trouble."

Brown was motivated, at least in part, to raise money to post bond for her boyfriend, awaiting trial for burglary in Blackford County.

A member of her traveling party in Florida had been one of her boyfriend's codefendants. About twenty-four hours before her death, Brown told police that man had threatened her life.

Her report put that man at or near the top of a list of several suspects in the homicide.

However, when police announced they had solved the case, more than five years later in March 2015, it was another man who was charged with killing Brown—Danny Lee Saintignon Jr., then thirty-three, facing counts of murder, robbery and conspiracy to commit burglary.

Saintignon at the time was serving a twenty-three-year prison term for his role in a 2013 armed home invasion at a Muncie couple's west-side apartment.

(His father, Danny Saintignon Sr., had pleaded guilty to murder in 2010 after DNA tests linked him to the 1989 rape and murder of a sixty-eight-year-old woman in her Indianapolis home.)

When the younger Saintignon stood trial in Delaware Circuit Court 3, in October 2017, a codefendant testified the defendant had enlisted him in a plot to steal prescription medications from Brown's home.

The man, and another witness, also said Saintignon had later confessed to fatally stabbing Brown.

In her closing argument to jurors, defense attorney Jill Gonzalez acknowledged her client had behaved less than admirably in his personal relationships with women. But she maintained there was not sufficient evidence to convict her client of killing Brown.

"Being an ass doesn't make you a murderer," she said.

After two weeks of testimony, the jury deliberated for about an hour before finding Saintignon guilty of the murder, robbery and burglary charges.

He was also convicted of conspiracy to commit obstruction of justice, based on testimony he arranged for a fellow prison inmate to warn a prosecution witness, via Facebook, to not cooperate with the homicide investigation.

In a sentencing memorandum, Eric Hoffman, then chief deputy prosecutor, wrote that Saintignon was "truly the proverbial monster lurking in the darkness who plots and plans to attack and violate other human beings."

At Saintignon's sentencing hearing on January 4, 2018, Hoffman—later that year to be elected Delaware County prosecutor—noted the defendant

DECEMBER 24, 2009

Local news: A bird-frightening system that cost nearly $40,000 was successful in persuading thousands of birds to stop congregating in downtown Muncie, officials said.

Music: Topping the *Billboard* Hot 100 was "Empire State of Mind" by Jay-Z and Alicia Keys.

TV: *American Idol, Dancing with the Stars* and *NCIS* were the TV season's most popular programs.

Movies: *The Blind Side*, released on November 20, remained the nation's most popular movie.

Books: *I, Alex Cross* by James Patterson was the top-selling fiction book in the United States.

had told a probation officer he was a "retired" member of the Aryan Brotherhood prison gang.

"I don't know if you get a pension with that or not," said Hoffman, drawing an enraged reaction from Saintignon.

"That's because you're stupid!" the convicted killer said. "You need to do your research."

The outburst prompted two men—one the father of Monica Brown's two youngest children—to comment. The handcuffed and shackled defendant rose to his feet and turned to face his antagonists, seated near him in the courtroom gallery.

Saintignon cursed and asked, "What are you going to do about it?"

The men then appeared to lunge in the direction of Saintignon but were held back by their friends as court security officers, one holding an electronic shock device, quickly moved in.

The two spectators left the courtroom under their own power. One later said he "just wanted to get my hands around [Saintignon's] neck."

The hearing's only witness was Brown's daughter Kimberly, who tearfully recounted the devastating impact the 2009 murder had on her family,

"I will never be OK," Brown said. "And I will never wake up from this nightmare. This is my reality."

Judge Linda Ralu Wolf imposed a maximum sentence of 137 years and six months.

With credit for good behavior, Saintignon will be eligible for release in August 2095, when he would be 114.

THE COLD CASE SQUAD

All over the country, headlines note retired police investigators who come back, on a part-time basis, to reopen cold cases and try to close some long-outstanding, unsolved homicides.

"Cold case squads" have become well-known thanks to podcasts and articles. But could a cold case squad be formed in Delaware County, Indiana, home to dozens of unsolved murders, among them the cases featured in this book?

One of the best-known retired investigators on the national scene is Paul Holes, who had a suspect in the case of the East Area Rapist, also known as the Golden State Killer, but couldn't close the case before he retired from the Contra Costa County sheriff's office in March 2018.

Holes most famously traded information with Michelle McNamara, a veteran internet crime writer who wrote the book *I'll Be Gone in the Dark* about the home invader, rapist and killer she called the Golden State Killer.

McNamara contacted Holes, who was working in a second career as an investigator in the Contra Costa County prosecutor's office, about the Golden State Killer.

Holes told Oxygen.com in 2020 that he was nervous about sharing information with McNamara, particularly the concern that McNamara might release the information. When she did not in the early months of their conversations, Holes came to trust her. *I'll Be Gone in the Dark* was published two years after McNamara's death.

Ultimately, a suspect who police believe was the Golden State Killer was arrested thanks to DNA matching.

Longtime investigator Jerry Cook. *Photo by Keith Roysdon.*

Around 2020, retired Delaware County sheriff's deputy and veteran investigator Jerry Cook contacted Delaware County sheriff Tony Skinner about several former investigators coming back to go over files of outstanding cold cases. Cook followed his time as a police officer with a decade and a half as an investigator in the Delaware County prosecutor's office.

Cook recounted for the first time for this book about his idea for a cold case squad.

"There were a few of us old investigators who were still around," Cook said, naming several of them, including one former investigator who was interviewed for this book but declined to speak publicly, citing the potential for danger to his family.

Cook proposed to Skinner that the former cops look through old case files and try to close some cases.

Cook said Skinner reacted positively, but the two talked about how it could legally be done: whether the retired investigators could be appointed as reserve deputies—which would require that they be trained and tested— or named special deputies. Either way, they would need to have some legal authority to look through files and interview witnesses or even suspects.

Then the idea languished until 2022, when Cook mentioned it in interviews for this book. Cook and the other retired investigator who asked not to be named met at a Bob Evans restaurant in Muncie in the fall of 2022.

Cook noted that he'd never heard back from Skinner, following up on the idea of a cold case squad.

In an interview for this book, Skinner confirmed that the idea had fallen by the wayside.

"Jerry did approach me," Skinner said. "I have not talked to anybody about that.

"I would still be interested in exploring that option," the sheriff added.

Sadly, Cook said he was, two years after the fact, no longer able to take on that role.

"I don't have time to do it anymore." At seventy-three, Cook was, in late 2022, still active, overseeing security for Ivy Tech Community College's campuses in Delaware County.

"We all talked about it at one time," Cook said about the other retired investigators. "We were all interested. We thought it would be a good idea.

"Those guys [the investigators] have the expertise and the training to do that.

"It's free help, for god's sake."

Wanting to keep his hand in law enforcement and investigations is a simple matter for Cook.

"I don't want to sit at home in a rocking chair," he said.

Is a cold case squad in Delaware County's future? It's hard to say. But veteran officers and investigators say it could help close the books on dozens of unsolved murders.

Because Delaware County has no shortage of cold cases.

BIBLIOGRAPHY

Introduction

CBS News. "Crime Without Punishment." June 2022.
Interviews by the authors.
Personal observation of August 2014 scene search and subsequent interviews.

Assassination

News coverage from Muncie newspapers, October 1962.
Walker, Douglas, and Keith Roysdon. "Who Killed Maggie Mae Fleming." *Star Press*, November 27, 2011.

"We Know He Did It. We Just Can't Prove It"

Interviews by the authors.
Project Cold Case. www.projectcoldcase.org.
Roysdon, Keith, and Douglas Walker. *The Westside Park Murders*. Charleston, SC: The History Press, 2021.

A Young Mother's Brutal Slaying

Garrett, Eric. *Unprosecuted: My Mother's Murder and the Search for Accountability*. Milwaukee, WI: Genius Books, 2020.
Interviews by the authors.
Roysdon, Keith, and Douglas Walker. "33 Years Later, Murdered Woman's Son Wants Justice." *Star Press*, August 7, 2014.

A Daughter Remembers

Interviews by the authors.
Roysdon, Keith, and Douglas Walker. "Father's Murder Haunts Children for 40 Years." *Star Press*, August 11, 2013.

Murder at the Maples Motel

Interviews by the authors.
Roysdon, Keith, and Douglas Walker. "Who Killed Lou Ann Cox." *Star Press*, November 20, 2011.

Death on "the Corner"

Interviews by the authors.
Roysdon, Keith, and Douglas Walker. "Who Killed Bill Gump?" *Star Press*, November 27, 2011.
Various articles about "The Corner," *Muncie Star* and *Muncie Evening Press*, various dates.

Stairway to Heaven

Interviews by the authors.
Roysdon, Keith, and Douglas Walker. "Who Killed Joni Brooks." *Star Press*, September 15, 2013.

A Civil War Veteran's Slaying Goes Unsolved

Interviews and research by the authors.
Muncie and Indianapolis newspaper articles, various dates, September 1898.

Holiday Homicide

Interviews by the authors.
Roysdon, Keith, and Douglas Walker. "Who Killed Ruby Dean Moore." *Star Press*, December 8, 2013.

A Need to See Justice Done in His Son's Murder

Interviews by the authors.
Roysdon, Keith, and Douglas Walker. "Who Killed Sebastian Cisneros." *Star Press*, Sunday, December 11, 2011.

"I Dream I See Blood"

Interviews by the authors.
Roysdon, Keith, and Douglas Walker. "Who Killed Ray Pinnick." *Star Press*, December 2, 2012.

Running with Some Bad People

Roysdon, Keith, and Douglas Walker. "Who Killed Pete Journay." *Star Press*, December 2, 2012.

The Murder Season of 1979

Interviews by the authors.
Muncie Evening Press and *Muncie Star* coverage, various days for three killings, March through May 1979.
Roysdon, Keith, and Douglas Walker. *The Westside Park Murders*. Charleston, SC: The History Press, 2021.

Cold Case Farm

Interviews by the authors.
Roysdon, Keith, and Douglas Walker. "Who Killed Charles Frank Graham." *Star Press*, January 26, 2014.
Various articles in the *Muncie Star* and *Muncie Evening Press*, August and September 1988.

"He Needs to Be Held Accountable"

Interviews by the authors.
Roysdon, Keith, and Douglas Walker. "Who Killed Crystal Sedam." *Star Press*, April 5, 2015.

"If the Tables Were Turned and I Were Murdered"

Interviews by the authors.
Roysdon, Keith, and Douglas Walker. "Who Killed Garth Rector." *Star Press*, May 22, 2016.

"I Want Them to Sit in Prison Until the Day They Die"

Interviews by the authors.
Roysdon, Keith, and Douglas Walker. "Who Killed William Gene Burton." *Star Press*, August 5, 2014.

A Muncie Mother Goes Missing

Interviews by the authors.

The Killing of "Bobby Blue"

Roysdon, Keith, and Douglas Walker. "Who Killed Robert Nelson." *Star Press*, January 10, 2016.

Who's Got the Files?
The Absence of Records Hampers Cold Case Reviews

Interviews by the authors.
Roysdon, Keith, and Douglas Walker. *The Westside Park Murders*. Charleston, SC: The History Press, 2021.
Various reports of flooding in local government buildings.

The Killing of James Tricker Jr.

Research by the authors.

"What Goes Around..."

Roysdon, Keith, and Douglas Walker. "Who Killed Cecil John Carter?" *Star Press*, August 10, 2014.

"The Proverbial Monster Lurking in the Darkness"

Roysdon, Keith, and Douglas Walker. "Who Killed Monica 'Nikki' Brown." *Star Press*, December 24, 2011.
———. "Felon Charged in 2009 Murder." *Star Press*, March 31, 2015.

The Cold Case Squad

Interviews by the authors.
McNamara, Michelle. *I'll Be Gone in the Dark*. New York: HarperCollins, 2018.
Tron, Gina. "A 'Big Switch for Me': Golden State Killer Investigator Paul Holes Revelas Why He Trusted Michelle McNamara." True Crime Buzz, July 17, 2020. Oxygen.com.

INDEX

ABOUT THE AUTHORS

Veteran journalist Douglas Walker has covered the criminal justice system in East-Central Indiana for most of the past four decades. For more than thirty-five years, he has served in reporting and editing roles for the *Star Press* and its predecessor, the *Muncie Evening Press*.

Walker has received dozens of awards for writing, investigative reporting and public service from state, regional and journalism organizations. Many have been the result of his collaborations with reporter Keith Roysdon, with whom he also wrote a weekly column on Muncie politics for many years. This marks the duo's fourth book on crime and justice in Muncie and Delaware County.

The Ball State University graduate is an eighth-generation resident of the Muncie area. Through his reporting, Walker has taken his readers to hundreds of crime scenes, scores of murder trials, two presidential inaugurations and more than thirty election nights as well as into the death chamber at the Indiana State Prison for an eyewitness account of an execution.

Walker is married (Jennifer) and has three children, three stepchildren and eight grandchildren.

Keith Roysdon is a lifelong Indiana resident who now lives in Tennessee. He began his career at Muncie, Indiana newspapers while he was still in high school in November 1977. He won more than thirty state and national first-place awards for journalism, many of them for work cowritten by Douglas Walker. Their third true crime book, *The Westside Park Murders*, was named Best Nonfiction Book of 2021 by the Indiana Society of Professional Journalists.

Roysdon's crime novel *Seven Angels* won the 2021 Hugh Holton Award for Best Unpublished Novel from Mystery Writers of America Midwest. He writes news and pop culture articles for several websites and also writes fiction. He and his wife, Robin, are the proud parents of a son, James.